SUCCESS
SECRETS OF
SACRAMENTO'S
BUSINESS
PROFESSIONALS™

TZEDAKAH
PUBLICATIONS

Second Printing
September 1990

Cover design ©
1990 by Tzedakah
Publications

Cover & Interior
Design by Craig
Johnson

Produced by Green
Mountain Graphics

NOTE: Although the author and publisher have researched all sources to ensure the accuracy and completeness of the information contained in this book, we assume no responsibility for errors, inaccuracies, omissions or any other inconsistency herein. Any slights against people or organizations are unintentional. Furthermore, the author and publisher specifically disclaim all warranties, express or implied with respect to defects in information included in this book, and/or the business techniques and advice described in this book, and in no event shall the author or publisher be liable for any loss of profit or any other commercial damage, including but not limited to special, incidental, consequential or other damages.

PUBLISHED IN THE UNITED STATES OF AMERICA

A trademark application for registration of the words, Success Secrets™ of Sacramento's Business Professionals, has been submitted to the U.S. Patent and Trademark Office. Tzedakah Publications is a subsidiary of Executive Strategy Inc. (ESI), 3100 Fite Circle, Suite 106, Sacramento, California 95827, (916) 369-1001.

Library of Congress Cataloging in Publication Data

Cawthorn, David L.

Success Secrets™ of Sacramento's Business Professionals, Volume I

90-070332

ISBN 0-929999-01-0

Business/Motivational

I would like to express my gratitude to the many people who contributed to the writing, editing and production of this book. These include the partici‑ pants themselves, who proofed and edited portions of their chapters; Sue Robertson and Cassaundra Cawthorn, who spent hundreds of hours transcribing interview tapes; Dolores Gap Hoffman, production artist with Green Mountain Graphics; and Nancy Curley, who proofed the final galleys.

I would especially like to thank my business associ‑ ates Dave Putnam, Dan Leacox and Brent Leacox for their superb management of this project; Craig Johnson for his persistence in fine-tuning the page layout and cover design; Barrett McBride whose editorial skills enhanced many of the thoughts presented in this book; and Laura Walker, an exceptionally skilled and understanding editor, whose input greatly increased the readability of this volume.

I owe a special debt of gratitude to Alan Gold, the first person I talked to about this concept, who coura‑ geously told others about the project and was my staunchest supporter along the way; and Laurie Litt, who assisted in contacting appropriate people to be featured in this book.

Last, but not least, I would like to thank my wife, Iris, whose words of encouragement kept me up when I was down.

This book is dedicated to American entrepreneurs throughout the ages —from the Henry Fords, J. Paul Gettys and P.T. Barnums of yesteryear to the Ted Turners, Steve Jobses and Donald Trumps of today. Most of all, it's dedicated to our readers—the business superstars of tomorrow.

As president of Executive Strategy Inc. (ESI), a Sacramento marketing, advertising and design firm, I meet and get to know many successful business professionals. In the course of doing business with them, I've discovered that local commerce is rich with dynamic individuals who are making their mark on Sacramento's legacy. Their stories are both provocative and inspirational, and I felt this wealth should be shared.

The participants featured in the book were selected as those rare individuals who organize a business undertaking, assuming the risk for the sake of profit, and make it happen. They are men and women to be admired, emulated and appreciated, for in no other segment of society can the essence of America's great free enterprise system be seen more clearly.

Therefore, it is with a high spirit of appreciation that I present to you twenty business men and women who deserve our lavish praise for their accomplishments. And our thanks for sharing their secrets of success with us.

David Cawthorn
April 1990
Sacramento, California

Gary Armlin is the president of Sunrise Vista Mortgage Corporation. Formerly, he was a real estate agent for Century 21, where he quickly earned membership in the prestigious Masters Club. He later became a loan officer at Statewide City Mortgage in Sacramento before founding his own company. He has an Associate of Arts degree in business and real estate from American River College and is currently pursuing a bachelor's degree in economics and finance at CSUS.

A t twenty-eight, Gary Armlin is in the midst of his second solo venture in the real estate industry. Gary began his career as a real estate agent for the Century 21 system, where he steadily grossed more than two million dollars in annual sales. Realizing that there were other lucrative aspects of the real property business, Gary moved on to mortgage banking and eventually to his own company—Sunrise Vista Mortgage Corporation—which represents more than one hundred firms in the lending industry.

Armlin is highly motivated and has both a plan and a definite strategy for the growth of Sunrise Vista. Much of his success can be traced to the level of technology he has introduced into the business. For example, he brought in a computer expert who is very well known for his software applications in the field of mortgage banking. This programmer has developed a leading-edge system for simultaneously tracking the complex mortgage loan process on hundreds of open cases.

Armlin's innovative methods and hands-on approach have brought him loyal clients who know they can count on him to find the right loan to fit their needs.

Work is at the top of the priority list for Gary and his wife, Debbie, who is also in the mortgage business as vice-president of a local firm. They are similar to many ambitious, young, professional couples today who work long hours and rarely find time for relaxation. As Gary points out, the business is booming now and the market is hot, so this is the time to put energy into building for the future.

Armlin is rapidly setting up the organization needed to propel him into the megamillion dollar volume he hopes to achieve within five years.

"...books gave me the confidence I needed to relate to people of all ages and back- grounds."

"Honesty and money are not incompatible..."

Author's Note: *Perfectly groomed and smartly dressed, Armlin projects an essence of coolness as he leans forward on his well-organized desk. His flashing brown eyes and quick smile declare that all is under control. Our interview evolved nicely as the savvy salesman extolled the virtues of his product, smoothly and deliberately. Young, smart and articulate...my first and lasting impressions of Gary Armlin.*

I didn't start out in real estate. My previous career was almost as far from the property selling game as you can get—photography!

I worked as a photographer's assistant when I first came to Sacramento, and, through a succession of jobs, became a full-fledged photographer. I really enjoyed it. It was creative, fun and potentially lucrative, but it seemed to lack something I vitally needed.

After a year and a half, I gave up the camera to seek something more substantial. My search landed me in real estate school, where I accelerated my learning schedule and got through the course in six weeks. The next day I was selling houses!

LISTEN AND LEARN

I went to work for a top real estate firm and got my first check thirty-three days later. This was only thirty-three days after I was licensed. I had no intention of waiting the "six months to a year" everyone was telling me about. I was driven.

It was then I looked around and realized that the people who were telling me to be patient were not the agents who were successful. I promptly quit listening to the skeptics and started watching the brokers who were moving the properties.

In my first eight months I became the number three producer in my office. In the next full year I became the top producer in the office, as well as number three in the company for the entire Northern California region.

The one element to which I attribute my quick success is listening to and watching the right people.

SELF-HELP LEADS TO CONFIDENCE

What I lacked in experience, I made up for by reading informative books and attending seminars. I have read all the Tom Hopkins books, the Zig Ziglar book, and many books by lesser known authors.

I found that just reading the books won't magically make you a great salesperson, however. You have to put the knowledge to work. There's a large group of real estate agents who read the books and go to the seminars, but that's all they do. They don't apply what they learn. I did. Also, I wasn't afraid to go out and put those ideas to work.

Those books gave me the confidence I needed to relate to people of all ages and backgrounds. Many other agents my age were intimidated by these people, but I just dove right in. I knew I had trained as well as I could train, I had read as much as I could read, and I was honest. I figured with those factors on my side, people would believe in me and trust me. And they did.

MIXING MONEY AND MORALS

Many people perceive real estate salespeople as dishonest—"They're just out for a buck" is what some people say. Unfortunately, there may be some truth to that when describing some of the agents and brokers.

Honesty and money are not incompatible, however. When I was selling, if I was unable to answer a client's question, I had no problem telling him so. I've always felt honesty to be the best policy.

ENTER THE MORTGAGE BANKER

I enjoyed selling real estate, with one exception—financing the sales had become increasingly frustrating. There was no help for the agents on the financial side. In 1986, I decided to take my knowledge to mortgage banking to address a need in the industry that wasn't being properly met.

I learned the mortgage banking business at a local mortgage company, which was the largest independent company in Sacramento at the time. I worked there for almost two years as a loan officer, and I really enjoyed it. I was able to learn the ropes very quickly because it was

"In 1986, I decided to take my knowledge to mortgage banking to address a need in the industry that wasn't being properly met."

"...I began to see the need for a competent person out on the street assisting the real estate industry with facts, honesty and just hard work."

at the height of the 1986 buying craze. Interest rates had dropped to eight percent and this development encouraged many people to refinance and others to purchase.

In addition, housing prices began to go up in Sacramento so investors were buying more. I was one little guy taking as many applications as I could and doing the best job possible with them. My only choice was to learn quickly!

RUSHING THROUGH RESOURCES

As with real estate sales, I jumped in and tried to learn all I could as fast as I could. I read all the memos, all the manuals and got as much advice as I could from others in the industry.

Too often I find that people don't take advantage of all the resources out there. That's a mistake. You can learn by just doing the job and hoping it comes to you through experience, but you can also push the limits a little and acquire knowledge from others who have already had the experience. That is common sense stuff, but you'd be surprised how many people don't do it.

I could have gone to a mortgage banking academy, but I know many people who have attended them and they only know textbook theory.

By speaking to the pros, I believe I have a much broader vision of what's happening. I don't always know every detail, no one does. But I think I see the big picture a lot better than most.

PERSPECTIVES ON SUCCESS FROM GARY ARMLIN
- Self-help works only if you work at it
- Ethics and business
- Superheated Sacramento home market
- Personal-business balance
- Don't burn bridges

BECOMING AN AGENT'S BEST FRIEND

Once I felt confident with my expertise, I began to see the need for a competent person out on the street assisting the real estate industry with facts, honesty and just hard work. For that reason, I left the safety of my job to form my own company, Sunrise Vista Mortgage Company. We originate loans—conventional, FHA and VA.

The advantage of using my company over a direct seller is the number of options we can offer. I deal with over one hundred different companies, so I am more likely to find the perfect loan match for the customer.

Also, I am not paid according to the interest rate. I make the same amount of money whether the loan goes through for eight percent or twelve percent—it doesn't matter. I am simply paid a predetermined origination fee. This agreement works better for the consumer.

I have also worked to develop sales tools to help the agents. For example, I can use my computer facilities to create listing fliers, and provide loan comparisons at a moment's notice. My customers find me available at all hours and I do a solid, confident job.

All those extras have paid off. Since starting my business, I have attracted a group of agents who are very loyal to me, and I work with them, as well as through their referrals.

"The biggest obstacle I face is trying to please everyone."

THE PERSONAL TOUCH

The biggest obstacle I face is trying to please everyone. It's sometimes difficult to please your customers, the agents and the government, if you're dealing with a government loan. As home prices rise, so does the disappointment level, with many people unable to get the homes they want.

Personally I feel I sometimes take too much interest in individual clients and their situations. There have been times when my entire commission went to close a loan—just to get somebody into a house. My friends and family say, "You know, you may be going a little too far," but I believe you'll always be successful if you really care.

PRICES CONTINUE TO SOAR

I think Sacramento is going to follow very closely the patterns of San Jose, San Diego and Los Angeles. Those cities each had a ten-to-twelve-year race to the moon with their prices.

The political scene is one determinant of the real estate market—how much growth the supervisors and the city councils will allow. We have the land and the room to grow in all directions. Where there's land, there's going to be somebody who owns it and wants to subdivide it.

If we can control the traffic and all the internal problems that are contiguous with growth, we will

"The political scene is one determinant of the real estate market—how much growth the supervisors and the city councils will allow."

continue to grow for about five to seven years. After that, we are probably going to see some leveling off around the mid-90s.

REWARDS COME IN ALL SIZES

On a daily basis, the rewards of my own business are the thank yous. Then I have my own personal, little victories. Perhaps it's getting a loan approved or installing a new computer program, or buying a new picture for the wall. Every little victory indicates that my business is growing.

My big rewards will be realized in the future when I will be able to look back and say, "I built this from zero and look at it today!"

I don't want to be huge, though. I want to grow in the next two years to be about twelve times the size I am now—to become a two hundred million dollar company within three to five years and maintain that level through the 1990s.

DAMN THE COMPUTERS, FULL SPEED AHEAD

Two hundred million isn't an unrealistic goal because I've taken the time from the beginning to build the foundation. I have purposely built my mortgage loan business at a very slow pace in order to have a solid foundation of modernization and automation. In my opinion my computer system is the best one in existence for mortgage banking. I've developed all the tools that are necessary for a two hundred million dollar company. Unlike the companies that are always behind, trying to catch up, I can have a fast, straight, smooth line to the top.

Computers are a tool, not a solution by themselves. Many company administrators believe that buying a system is going to be the answer to all their problems. But, of course, it's not. If you are aware of that fact, and you know exactly how you will use the technology, it can give you a huge edge over the competition. It reduces my staffing needs by about twenty-five percent and speeds up the paper process.

IF YOU'RE HAPPY, I'M HAPPY

Success is personal satisfaction. It's when I'm content and happy that I've done the best job with the tools I have available. It's making as many people happy as I can. When I've done my job and not stepped on other people to do it, I feel successful.

At times I wish I had more of that killer instinct that many so-called successful business people have. If I can make money without having to step on other people, though, I think I'm going to be more successful in the long run. That's my personal goal—to do it being a nice guy. Every person I've worked with is still my friend; I haven't burned any bridges.

My company is ready now to become much bigger, but I wonder—will it work at that larger level? Will I still be able to be the nice guy all the time? I don't know. As I deal with people every day who swindle and scam on everything from copy machines to loans, I wonder. Do I have to lower myself to their level to deal with them? It's not something I intend to do.

FOLLOWING UP

Probably the thing I have to fight the most is response time—returning my phone calls quickly. Sometimes it seems unfair that agents need everything immediately, but if I get a call at 4:59 and I really want to leave at 5:00, I have to handle that call. They need me now, and I can't wait until tomorrow morning because they might have a client sitting there now, ready to buy.

My loyal clients won't leave me. They're not going to find somebody else, but they're going to be upset because they needed me and I wasn't there. Therefore, the absolute rule is to return your calls and follow up, follow up, follow up!

SUCCESS HAS ITS PRICE

High stress is something I deal with on a daily basis. Sometimes I just have to get away. When those times hit me, I go to the ocean or maybe to Tahoe. It can be hard on my family too because, when I am over-stressed, I need to be alone.

The downside of running your own business is that it's hard to devote enough time to your personal life, and it bothers me that I can't spend more time with my wife. We have no children because we're afraid we don't have the essential time to devote to them. Unfortunately, I haven't yet come up with a solution to provide more of a balance, but we're working on it.

CARING IS A PERFECT KEY

Excellence in business means doing an effective job

"I want to grow in the next two years to be about twelve times the size I am now—to become a two hundred million dollar company within three to five years and maintain that level through the 1990s."

"The very first person

I hired...was a

computer expert."

regardless of the size of your company. It's being as good as you can be at that moment in time.

I'm a perfectionist, sometimes to my detriment. For example, I expect a letter to be free of typographical errors. I've dealt with companies who don't pay close attention to the details, and it affects their image with clients.

Anything that's worth doing is worth doing right. Take the time to check your spelling. Read through your letters. Read through everything at least twice. Caring is important. You have to make a conscious effort constantly to do the job correctly.

A PERSONAL APPROACH TO ADVERTISING

Advertising is something I do in subtle ways. I have a place on my database for every customer's birthday and the anniversary date of the closing on his or her transaction. Every week I send out anniversary cards. "It's the anniversary of your home. How's it going? Think about your real estate needs," that kind of thing.

Thoughtful, personal advertising is a growing gold mine. I think this personal approach is something that's not utilized nearly enough. So many people that you've done business with in the past don't follow up on you.

That's not the only answer to prospering. I see too many people looking for a single item to solve all their business problems. The computer's not it. Databases are not it. Attractive sales reps are not it. They're all a part of an intricate picture reliant on the creator to support it and make it grow.

Gary Armlin
Sunrise Vista Mortgage Corporation
6060 Sunrise Vista Dr., Suite 1270
Citrus Heights, CA 95610
Telephone: 916-721-0540
Fax: 916-721-0622

Gary X. Brown

Gary Brown *is the president of Gary Brown Enterprises, a company that specializes in concepting, organizing and marketing trade shows and business conferences throughout the United States. He was formerly the business and real estate editor of The Sacramento Union, special sections director of The Sacramento Bee and founder of two prominent magazines in Sacramento—Sacramento Magazine and Executive Place. He currently markets nine major projects, including Government Technology Conference, which is held in Sacramento, California; Albany, New York; and Austin, Texas.*

In his bestselling book *Megatrends,* John Naisbitt said, "The most important reason for the current entrepreneurial explosion in the United States, the huge growth in new small businesses (more than six hundred thousand new ones) is...that the new source of power is not money in the hands of a few, but information in the hands of many."

Knowledge drives our economy today, and nowhere can this trend be seen more clearly than in the trade show and conference industry, one of the fastest growing in the world.

Gary Brown, founder and president of Gary Brown Enterprises, saw this trend developing several years ago and began to carve out his niche in this lucrative market.

Brown founded several Home & Garden shows throughout Northern California, including the Sacramento Home & Garden show held at Cal Expo each year. He is also a founder and general partner in Government Technology Conference, the largest intergovernmental information event in the United States.

The annual May conference in Sacramento draws more than ten thousand people and provides educational seminars as well as the latest innovations from more than two hundred leading computer companies.

Brown considers his business enterprise somewhat of an entrepreneurial farm. He has helped many people get started and learn to successfully run a business in the trade show industry. Many of his former employees have become successful entrepreneurs in their own right.

Brown has been recognized by his associates as an entrepreneur's entrepreneur. Hanging prominently on a wall is a plaque presented to him from the staff of The Sacramento Bee. It reads, "Gary Brown, Magazine Mogul.

"If there is one key factor to my success and the growth of my business, it has been finding good people, taking their best skills and fitting them into the right area."

"I got my first

entrepreneurial twinge

as a reporter when I

was transferred from

the sports section to

the real estate and

business sections of

the Sacramento

Union."

Sunday Man, a magazine of The Sacramento Bee, February 13, 1981. **The Entrepreneur's Credo:** I do not choose to be a common man. It is my right to be uncommon...if I can. I seek opportunity...not security. I do not wish to be a kept citizen, humbled and dulled by having the state look after me. I want to take the calculated risk; to dream and to build; to fail and to succeed. I refuse to barter incentive for a dole; I prefer the challenges of life to the guaranteed existence; the thrill of fulfillment to the stale calm of Utopia. I will not trade freedom for beneficence nor my dignity for a handout. I will never cower before any master nor bend to any threat. It is my heritage to stand erect, proud and unafraid; to think and act for myself, to enjoy the benefit of my creations and to face the world boldly and say: This, with God's help, I have done. All this is what it means to be an entrepreneur."

Author's Note: If the city of Sacramento ever decides to appoint an ambassador of good will, I nominate Gary Brown. Born and raised in Sacramento, Gary exudes the friendly, gregarious personality of one who grew up in the slow-paced, overgrown cowtown that Sacramento once was. Gary is a large man with a great smile and a heart of gold. We met for his interview at his home in the Land Park area, where we enjoyed an afternoon of relaxing on his patio and reminiscing about the good ol' days.

I f there is one key factor to my success and the growth of my business, it has been finding good people, taking their best skills and fitting them into the right area.

From the beginning, when I hired employees, they were given the opportunity to work with my proven track record. They could utilize all the resources of our company—support staff, advertising, PR and management of the facilities. All they had to do was sell exhibit space for trade shows. Everything else was handled.

I have allowed people to be something more than nine-to-fivers, and we all long for that. It's a freedom. I believe that no matter what we do, we will rise to the highest level we can attain.

Several of my employees have been very successful. Many have earned $30-$40,000 for six months of work, became part-owners of a show and eventually bought me out!

The potential of part-ownership was always the motivation to keep them here, to make them work hard, and to make them overlook the fact they weren't getting rich to start off with. It worked for them and it worked for me. That's how my business grew.

GAINING CONFIDENCE

I got my first entrepreneurial twinge as a reporter when I was transferred from the sports section to the real estate and business sections of the Sacramento Union. It was a different world. Having originally thought I would be a career journalist and retire with the gold watch at age 65, dealing with the business world became a real fascination to me.

The interesting people I met and the places I traveled to opened up a whole new world. I can remember meeting Alex Spanos; flying in his private Cessna Jet and listening to his own story of success. It was a real motivator.

While it was a very scary thought—this plunge into the business world on my own—I concluded: "If *they* can do it, why can't I?" It was rather naive thinking, I agree, but without dreaming nothing happens.

MAKING CONCESSIONS

My first venture into the business world was ownership of a private concession business. I had been doing public relations for several years on speedways and drag strips and saw there was a lot of food and beverage consumed at these events. One location in particular, now known as Sacramento Raceway, did not have an established concessionaire.

So, I took my first leave of absence from the Union (you could have one year and then return to the newspaper if you so desired) and decided to be a hot dog and soda mogul.

"A group of race promoters wanted to throw a national meet at this location and they were looking for somebody to promote the event. In order to cover my investment in the concession business, I became the drag strip promoter..."

"I had very little capital to get the magazine started, but borrowed money from bowling partners, real estate friends and neighbors."

I hired neighbors on weekends and launched this enterprise with one thousand dollars, nearly all of which went into inventory for the very first event of the year. There was no running water or electricity, but I met an old carnival barker by the name of Tuffy Johnson who had been in the concession business for years. He had a number of old modified concession wagons on his property that had virtually rusted through. But with some spit and polish, I made them do. Tuffy tried to convince me that the concession business wasn't one for the faint hearted and that I would get sick of it quick. He was right. I barely survived and had to eat most of my left-overs!

The owner of the drag strip died suddenly and it looked as though the entire operation would go under. But a group of race promoters wanted to throw a national meet at this location and they were looking for somebody to promote the event. In order to cover my investment in the concession business, I became the drag strip pro-moter, along with the owner's widow, Betty Clark.

We had one of the largest races in the strip's history and more than thirty-two thousand people showed up that weekend. I sold everything in sight!

But, as old man Johnson told me, it was a tough way to make a buck. I later returned to the Union, content and secure with the weekly "grind" of real estate and business news.

LESSONS FROM SACRAMENTO MAGAZINE

Five years later, in 1974, I got the creative itch again and teamed up with Martin Cracchiolo—then an ad salesman for the Union—and we launched Sacramento Magazine. We had no experience, no money, no marketing plan; but suddenly we were magazine publishers!

We created a corporation and brought together a group of friends, business acquaintances, bowling part-ners, etc., and we were able to raise two hundred thou-sand dollars. Martin and I personally took second mort-gages on our houses and later thirds. I have long since realized that capitalization is the name of the game for new enterprises and you better have double the amount of working capital you think you need.

I was the magazine's publisher, which meant that I sold ads, wrote stories and coordinated the production. We began with a very talented staff of fourteen. And throughout the five-year period I owned the publication, several creative people joined the staff and later went on to bigger and better things. Some of the former staffers I remember most fondly include Bob Sylva, now a feature writer for The Sacramento Bee; Cynthia Waggoner, now in corporate communications for the Shaklee Corp.; Carol Gage, who owns a communications firm locally; John Corcoran of the Corcoran Company in Sacramento; Dane Henas, owner of Henas Design here; and Gary Benjamin of Benjamin and Jamison, a San Francisco-based agency.

Sacramento Magazine was a great idea but it was premature and undercapitalized. We couldn't do the big slick publicity jobs. It was a good product, though, and we had some good months. One issue did $125,000 in ad sales. I'd never seen a magazine do that.

The main problem was keeping the good people I had hired. It was somewhat of a training base. My employees would attain a certain level of skill and somebody would say, "Gee, that guy's dynamite!" Someone else could always offer them more than I could. So as the farm team grew up and became major league rookies, they were picked off by people who could offer more benefits and higher salary. I didn't blame them for that, but it became frustrating.

"As the farm team grew up and became major league rookies, they were picked off by people who could offer more benefits and higher salary."

PERSPECTIVES ON SUCCESS FROM GARY BROWN
- Raising entrepreneurs
- Rookies on the block
- The winning formula
- Expanding the concept
- Working for the homeless
- Creating a happy medium

I think that's why it was hard to keep things going at Sacramento Magazine. It seemed as though every time we reached a certain point, we'd have to start all over with a bunch of rookies who had to be trained. Our ad sales would go down.

Sacramento Magazine was the most stressful time I've ever had in my life, because several times the printer called to say, "We're not going to print until you send us another $5,000." We always managed to make it by juggling things around. I gained tremendous knowledge in financial management and handling multiple priorities.

"Sacramento

Magazine was the

most stressful time I've

ever had in my life

because several times

the printer called to

say, "We're not going

to print until you send

us another $5,000."

DIVING IN AGAIN

As stressful as the Sacramento Magazine experience was, it wasn't too long after that I came up with another idea and plunged right in.

It was 1980 and Sacramento's business population was starting to emerge. I felt the newspapers weren't covering business extensively enough. There were no business publications, not even a business journal.

The first product of my focus on business was an annual handbook. I produced it for six years and ran it out of my trunk. It always did well—it was called the *Sacramento Business Handbook.* SACTO (Sacramento Area Commerce and Trade Organization) was my sponsor and circulation base. They supplied most of the information and research. We started to progress with this handbook and it was quite profitable. I was the publisher and Jack Woodard was the editor. We finally sold it when I began to get heavily involved with the trade shows.

AN EXECUTIVE PLACE AHEAD OF ITS TIME

As more and more larger companies began to move into Sacramento, I added a monthly publication with a business focus—*Executive Place Magazine.*

I said, "It seems to me that there is an audience of twenty to twenty-five thousand business executives who have a need, and I think there are business people with products who need to reach them." Executive Place depicted an executive lifestyle and focus, something totally different from everything else. That was the part of the market I set out to capture, rather than the general audience that I had with Sacramento Magazine, where you're fighting newspapers, radio and television.

This magazine would be designed to reach the cream of the crop, which meant twenty thousand business professionals who earn $50,000 on the average. "If you just want that segment and that's your message, Mr. Mercedes Dealer or Mr. Commercial Bank Lender, then Executive Place is the perfect spot for your advertising," I would explain to them.

Again, I still think the idea is viable, but I was undercapitalized. I couldn't afford to pay good salespeople what they demanded. I gave it a whirl for two years and sold it to a consortium of real estate developers and other Sacramento area business people.

A STERLING OPPORTUNITY

Chapter Two—near bankruptcy again. But just before I sold Executive Place Magazine, a friend of mine, Jo Sterling of Sterling-Moore-Golden Advertising in Sacramento, approached me on a trade show idea. Again my magic formula was working. I didn't know anything about trade shows either. By taking a hard look at this emerging industry, I realized it might be the "bionic business." Where else can you start with very little capital, have no standing inventory, initiate deposit monies well in advance of a show, eliminate collection problems and operate with a minimal amount of labor?

As the first year of the Sacramento Home & Garden Show concluded and exhibitors were handing me deposits for the following year and demanding additional space, it *clicked*. I said, "Hey, this just might be what I want to do when I grow up!" I was forty-three at the time.

Today the Sacramento Home & Garden Show is the largest in Northern California, with forty-five thousand people attending last year.

SURVEY SECRETS

I approached the shows differently than I did the magazines. First, I hired a market research company to compile a survey. I got eight thousand people to complete it by giving away a trip to Hawaii. I then paid the market research company $3,500 for providing the questionnaire and statistical analysis.

I took the survey to an ad agency and said, "Here's our market. Build me a radio and television campaign." I used the same formula later when I started shows in Fresno, Bakersfield and Stockton. Having those surveys done and then having an agency handle the marketing have been valuable tools in making my shows successful. Booth space for next year's Sacramento Home & Garden Show is seventy-five to eighty percent sold sixty days after a show.

REWARDS OF THE SPIRIT

Eventually, I had established home and garden shows for various communities in Central California and the business continued to grow. I had finally tapped a successful formula and the exhibitors were writing up more business at my shows than some had done in three to four months

"Executive Place depicted an executive lifestyle and focus, something totally different from everything else."

"...capitalization is the

name of the game for

new enterprises and

you better have double

the amount of working

capital you think you

need."

of normal business operation.

I hired individuals who demonstrated the same entrepreneurial spirit I had. It became apparent later, however, that it's mighty tough for two captains to run the same ship. In some cases, I sold the projects to these young up and comers. Part of the delight of this business has been to watch a budding entrepreneur go through the system and become his or her own person. Today, shows in Stockton, Santa Rosa, Bakersfield, Alameda, Contra Costa and Modesto are operated by former partners of mine who have taken the GBE success formula and applied it to their own successful companies.

FROM GARDENING TO GOVERNMENT
With my business foundation finally secure in 1985, I was able to venture out even further into the trade show field, and I developed a business relationship with another entrepreneurial firm, GMW. This company was primarily in the publishing business, but it had strong attachments to state and local government through a variety of publications.

Since emerging technology was the gist of their editorial thrust, they asked, "Could a government technology conference make it in the trade show field?"

Well, that's all history now. Five years ago we joined forces and launched Government Technology Conference. It is now the largest intergovernmental conference and trade show concept in the United States. Based on the Sacramento show—now in its fourth year—the concept is being applied successfully in Albany, New York and Austin, Texas, two other conference sites.

Suddenly, we went from retail-oriented home and garden products to discussions with the presidents and vice-presidents of Apple Computer, IBM, Hewlett-Packard, 3M, Digital Equipment, Sun Micro and virtually the entire Who's Who of the computer world.

Gads! That's a long way from those days of hawking hot dogs and sodas on a drizzly day at Sacramento Raceway!

THE BOTTOM LINE
Due to some very fine people in my organization, I have been allowed the freedom to financially manage and create new ventures. Through the use of technology, I am able to maintain daily accountability over all shows, sales

and the financial position of the company. I do this on a daily basis. If you can avoid daily and weekly mistakes, the profit and loss statement at the end of the year takes care of itself.

I think the biggest mistake most companies make is not knowing their financial position on any given day. They go "by guess and by golly" until they get backed into a corner and have no room to maneuver. I'm a statistical freak. I drive my people crazy with paperwork. But it has kept us out of trouble and has been an essential ingredient in our growth and prosperity.

PLUSES AND MINUSES
There are some drawbacks to running a trade show these days. First, it's hard to get dates. Also, facilities are not large enough and we're busting at the seams. If you came into Sacramento it would be slim pickings. If you went to some other cities like San Diego or San Jose which have new facilities with a couple million square feet, that's a different story.

What I like about the trade show profession is the flexibility it offers in my lifestyle. It has been good to me. It allows me to do other things that I love. I'm a Sacramentan and I think it's important to put something back into the community. One of the things I enjoy is working with the homeless, which I've been doing for three years through the Food Closet. My wife and I are also involved in many other social ministry projects.

I am able to fit these activities into my schedule because I have my company organized to the point I have maximum flexibility. The reason, once again, is that I have good people working for me. I am finally at the point where I can hire good people and keep them by offering incentive to earn a substantial amount of money. That is something that we didn't have at the magazines. I have a great general manager and I have two excellent bookkeepers.

I could spend every day at the office and I'd find something to do. However, at fifty-two years old, I seek new challenges. It's good to know I have a staff I can depend on.

OVERCOMING ENTHUSIASM
The biggest hurdle I had to overcome wasn't getting the money to start the business, or adequate office space, or

"Today the Sacramento Home & Garden Show is the largest in Northern California. We had forty-five thousand people attend last year."

even finding the right personnel.

The biggest obstacle I had to overcome in building my current business was containing my enthusiasm. I wanted to do everything all at once. When I finally found something that worked, I was forty-two years old. I said, "Gee, this trade show business is really exciting!" I suddenly wanted to do fifty shows all over the place. Without waiting for one to finish I was ready to get into another. It got so that I wanted to do everything simultaneously. I started a home improvement trade show too early. It almost didn't get off the ground. I wanted to move too fast to make up for lost time. I felt like, "Gee, I wish I would have started this when I was thirty!"

I finally overcame the urge to move too fast. I realized I couldn't do it. You can only move so fast. I avoided the mistake a lot of people make.

A MEASURE OF SUCCESS

I want to create shows that have value for people. When they say, "This is the best value we've got going in the marketplace where we can exhibit, get exposure and sell merchandise. We want to come back here next year," that to me is a win-win situation.

It isn't the dollars necessarily. I think it's a situation where the client and the company can look at each other and say, "We've done well. This was a good experience. It was profitable for us. I hope it was profitable for you."

I feel that's why our shows have grown and been well supported. Exhibitors don't keep coming back year after year because you're a good guy.

THE BASIC FACTS OF LIFE

I have the best business partner in the world. She's my wife. She doesn't work full-time in the business but helps out occasionally. She's always there. "Honey, what is it? Is there something I can help you with? Do you need to talk about something?" she'll ask. She has the patience of Job and a great amount of wisdom. With that, she gives me a clear perspective, whether it's a personal problem or a business problem. Most of the time she's right on target.

The challenge in my life now is to find that happy medium between work, family and my spiritual life. Achieving this balance is the greatest success a business person can attain. I feel I'm making good progress!

Gary Brown
Gary Brown Enterprises
2214 21st Street
Sacramento, CA 95818
916-452-6203
916-452-6231

Karen Comisso

Karen Comisso
is president of Loredan Biomedical Inc., a physical rehabilitation research, development and manufacturing firm headquartered in Davis, California. She was formerly medical sales manager for a leading pharmaceutical firm where she managed sales of medical ultrasonic transducers worldwide. Ms. Comisso earned a bachelor's degree in psychology from West Virginia University and a master's degree in education from University of Pittsburgh.

Loredan Biomedical Inc. is a Davis-based firm that designs, manufactures and markets computerized equipment and software for testing and rehabilitation of muscular injuries.

Sales of the LIDO family of equipment, as Loredan calls its products, hit close to $20 million in 1989. The company plans to make a public stock offering in 1992, and a sales volume of $100 million is expected by the mid-1990s.

International demand for Loredan's products is already very strong. U.S. medical technology is recognized as the best in the world, and the LIDO is recognized as the most technologically advanced system. Germany is Loredan's biggest foreign customer, followed by Japan, Italy, Switzerland, France, Sweden and Saudi Arabia.

The LIDO equipment is an amalgamation of high technology—robotics, personal computers and exercise machines. Sensors and gears created for robots give the machines the ability to measure motion. Personal computers interpret the data. Components designed for exercise gear provide the mechanism to bring it all together.

This type of technology becomes increasingly valuable to physicians, attorneys and insurance companies when used as an evaluating tool. In addition to testing and treating muscular injuries, the LIDO can help spot phony back ailments by analyzing the patient's performance on the machine. With the ability to simulate the hand manipulation and adjustment that physical therapists typically provide to their patients, the LIDO frees up more time for therapists to treat additional injuries.

LIDO devices sell for between $15,000 and $60,000, and, with therapists charging up to $200 per session, the equipment can pay for itself in as few as eighteen months.

"If someone had told me five years ago that I would become the president of Loredan Biomedical, I'd have said they were crazy!"

"Malcolm, however, is

a great person for

strategy and for ideas,

and I could see he just

needed a partner to

carry out those ideas."

Approximately seventy percent of Loredan's sales are to physical therapists, who make up one of the fastest-growing professions in American medicine. Other clients include hospitals, occupational therapists, orthopedic surgeons, chiropractors and athletic trainers.

Much of Loredan's success can be traced to its president, Karen Comisso. Upon joining Loredan as sales director, Comisso boosted the company's marketing efforts to astounding levels by engineering a no-nonsense sales strategy.

Author's Note: *Entering the Loredan offices, one sees an unpretentious environment. No fountains. No fancy furniture. The sense is that Loredan has nothing to prove. Comisso greeted me in the reception area. She comes across as very warm, personable and down-to-earth. Thirty minutes into our interview, however, I discovered a tenacious toughness that is at the heart of her success.*

I f someone had told me five years ago that I would become the president of Loredan Biomedical, I'd have said they were crazy! I was hired in 1985 as national sales manager on the recommendation of one of Loredan's venture capital investors. Prior to my coming on board, Malcolm Bond—the founder, chairman and, for the past two years, my husband—had fired two previous sales managers.

As soon as I joined the company, I sat down with Malcolm and said, "Okay, tell me what you want to have accomplished. I'm here as a team player. What are your ideas? What are your goals? Where do you want to go with this company?"

At that point the company was not doing well, having had three consecutive months of no sales. Malcolm was almost ready to give up. He didn't want to let go, but he had limited business experience and couldn't see a way out.

Malcolm, however, is a great person for strategy and for ideas, and I could see he just needed a partner to carry out those ideas. So, he outlined what he wanted and I proceeded to carry his plans through. That was the beginning of a great team!

A HUMBLE START

I definitely have come a long way from my beginnings. I was born forty years ago in Camden, New Jersey. My parents separated when I was a baby and my mother remained on welfare throughout my elementary and high school years.

Fortunately, I had teachers who positively influenced me in those tough times. One of them, my second grade teacher, was a beautiful woman named Ms. Troll. I remember her so vividly—I wanted to be just like her. She took special interest in me, giving me a little money here and there for doing chores because she knew how poor we were.

And Bruce Smith, my music teacher, encouraged me to work hard for good grades, and later on influenced my decision to take the SAT tests and apply for college.

The best part of my childhood, however, was sharing it with my twin sister Sharon. She was my best friend, and we remain close today. Sharon is very much like me except that she didn't go to college right after high school. She is a college student now, however, and is very successful in her professional life. She runs the computer department for a large men's clothing chain in New Jersey.

Sharon married shortly after high school, but I had different plans. By the time I reached high school, I was determined to be like my teachers, and getting an education became a high personal priority. At age 17, I left home with five dollars in my pocket, hopped on a bus to West Virginia University and never looked back.

MY LIFE AS A THERAPIST

I graduated with a degree in psychology and went to work for a mental health center in Ohio. I was a therapist for an outpatient mental health facility that was attached to a hospital in Steubenville, Ohio.

My supervisor was a talented social worker who became a mentor for me. She taught me sensitivity and gave me the skills to listen to people, to empathize with their feelings and to help guide them in their real life situations.

"I was a state worker; a civil servant with little upward mobility and very little external reward for jobs well done."

"I was a wildcat, a

female, a blonde, and

I was not an engi-

neer."

A young patient was assigned to me. Her name was Pam and she had been in and out of state hospitals all her life. As I worked with Pam, I discovered that she originally had been labeled schizophrenic by her parents in an effort to pass over to the state the responsibility of caring for her.

Pam was later diagnosed as having cerebral palsy. With encouragement, I was sure she could achieve independence. So I began coaching her and I told her that what she really needed to do was find a job. She ultimately did just that. She later married, had children and today she is doing quite well.

Helping Pam was unquestionably a success for me, and I have benefited greatly from the experience.

PERSPECTIVES ON SUCCESS FROM KAREN COMISSO
- Common sense approach to people
- Sales career offers direct reward for hard work
- Attitude adjustment
- Selling to the Japanese
- Profit sharing attracts excellent employees
- Fund raising never stops

CHANGING THE STATUS QUO
Shortly after Pam left, I realized that I had led myself into a blind alley. I was a state worker; a civil servant with little upward mobility and very little external reward for a job well done. I certainly was not independent like Pam had become. Instead I felt the system I worked in was holding me back. The financial aspects of the job were particularly bleak. No matter what you did, you got the same $300 pay raise as the guy next to you who did very little.

In a similar way to Pam, my immediate environment was holding me back. I had to break out of it to achieve a new level of independence. Having no role models other than my teachers, I quit work and went back to school.

I was able to receive a full scholarship for graduate school at University of Pittsburgh, and I graduated with a master's degree in special education. It was the 1970s. People around me were thinking hard about life and the times. I did the same and came to realize that I believed in the American Dream.

It occurred to me that one form of independence was strongly linked to performance, and I became determined to enter the business world.

LEARNING THE BUSINESS
Right out of graduate school, I went to work for the electronics division of a leading pharmaceutical company. Initially, I was intoxicated with the great independence I had in this new job. Unfortunately, I was transformed into a hellion. My attitude was, "Hey, I pulled myself out of poverty in Camden, New Jersey and I just completed a master's degree funded by a scholarship. I've got a lot going for me."

However, my supervisor and colleagues at my new job were unimpressed. The fact is I was not performing at my job. I was a wildcat, a female, a blonde and I was not an engineer.

One day my boss said, "It isn't working out with you. You've got to straighten up and change or you're out of here!"

THE TURNING POINT
At first I couldn't believe it. I had come all this way and now I was blowing it. Today I look back on that little talk with my boss and I feel very grateful for what he said. In a way, he did for me what I did for Pam.

I had been given an opportunity here and now I had to perform. Within three months I completely turned myself around. I focused all my energies on my job. It really was a garbage job, one no one else wanted to do. But I took ownership of it. I was going to make sure that I did the job better than anyone else had ever done before. I started new programs. One included calling every one of the existing customers and saying, "Hi, I'm Karen. I work for your supplier and we really care about you." Almost immediately I turned around that portion of the business from a $500,000 liability to a profit center. Finally, I was performing!

My boss was pleased and actually said it was the best job that anybody had ever done. As a reward, I received more responsibility and increased independence. He assigned me to a job in sales and put me in charge of Japan, which was producing no revenue for the company.

"By the end of my first year on the job, Japan was generating $250,000 in sales."

"The company

ultimately failed, but

not before I had made

a name for myself in

the medical equipment

sales field. With only a

prototype, I generated

sales of more than one

million dollars!"

INTERNATIONAL EXPERIENCE

Japan was an interesting assignment. Back then, we did all of our sales internationally by telex. In the beginning, the Japanese made a mistake and communicated with me as Mr. K. Comisso. That mistake turned out to be in my favor, as the Japanese historically do not accept a female in business.

The telex communications were difficult to understand, but I was patient. It paid off. By the time they found out I was a woman, I had already won their confidence and the sales were growing. By the end of my first year on the job, Japan was generating $250,000 in sales. At that point, my boss began to take an interest in Japan, and one day he said, "Japan really has potential. We can't have a woman handling that territory!" I felt like quitting. But my boss gave me another territory nobody wanted—Europe.

I took on Europe with the same focus and tenacity as Japan. At the time, Europe accounted for less than five percent of the company's total sales. In one year on the job, Europe was generating forty-five percent of total sales!

IMPORTANT MOVES

Even as a child, I dreamed a lot of California. While in high school, images of California beaches I saw in movies continually ran through my mind.

In 1983, I heard of a start-up company in Sacramento, and I seized the opportunity to work there. The company ultimately failed, but not before I had made a name for myself in the medical equipment sales field. With only a prototype, I generated sales of more than one million dollars!

The keys to my success in sales eventually opened the door for me at Loredan.

MOVING THE MBAs OUT

When I arrived at Loredan, I had a huge challenge facing me—it wasn't to become president—it was to be the best sales manager I could be. Initially that meant doing everything from cleaning the bathrooms to emptying the trash.

We generated $1.2 million in sales in 1985—which also turned out to be the annual revenue figure that year.

Selling the product was not a problem because our

products are the best. Unfortunately, though, in that first year the company was experiencing some growth problems that I could see might eventually destroy it.

First of all, by trying to be a democratic leader and by giving his managers freedom, Malcolm ended up giving away a lot of his power to the MBAs that we had hired. I could see they were trying to position themselves to move Malcolm out. That often happens in start-up companies. Once the venture capital comes in, the founders are usually gone within two years because, as inventors, they often lack business sense.

Fortunately, Malcolm is a quick study and realized that he had to regain his position of control before the business went under. We were operating in the red. Sales had slowed down because we couldn't get products out the door fast enough. Our research and development department wasn't producing products fast enough and we couldn't get our software developed fast enough.

Malcolm finally said, "I've had enough of this. I'm going to fire the whole team and start over again. I can't take this. Either I'm going to leave the company and let the venture capital people take over or we're going to do this ourselves."

I believed in Malcolm and the company so I knew together we could make this company successful.

"We are the Mercedes of the industry."

BLACK MONDAY

On "Black Monday" in 1986, Malcolm fired his entire MBA management team, including the president, and we began building our own successful team. It was a difficult decision to make because it impacted so many people, but we knew the company's survival was at stake.

Fortunately, the venture capital group applauded Malcolm's move because they finally saw Malcolm stand up for himself and take back control of his company.

COMPLEMENTARY ROLES

Today, my role as president is to handle the operations. I do the hiring and firing and basically run the company, but I'm taking Malcolm's ideas and carrying them through.

People look up to Malcolm and know that he's the real leader of the company—the visionary—but people look to me when they want a decision made. They look to me to find out how much money they can spend and

"It was always part of

Malcolm's dream to

share the company with

the employees..."

all of the other daily decisions.

Together, as a team, we successfully run what has become a multimillion dollar business, where the sky is the limit!

MAKING A MERCEDES

For my part, I took many of the principles I learned at the pharmaceutical firm and successfully applied them to Loredan. I attribute much of the company's success to customer service and constant customer contact.

We are the Mercedes of the industry. We offer the latest and the greatest in rehabilitation equipment. We strive to be first with the latest software and technology. We are extremely service-oriented. Our goal has been to position ourselves as the highest quality provider, giving our customers the most education. I believe we have succeeded. In fact, a well-known medical marketing research firm ranked us first in service.

We were also the first to add a clinical specialist to our staff. The clinical specialist is a physical therapist who is actually employed by the company. We use that highly qualified person to train our customers to use the product. Most companies send their sales reps or a videotape or the customer has to travel somewhere to get trained.

It's very expensive, but we actually go out to our customers three times for training. They recognize the value of it because we can train their entire staff simultaneously.

We also offer a seminar series in various parts of the world. In 1990 we're having one in Williamsburg, Virginia. Next we will be in Palm Desert, then Hong Kong and Dusseldorf. We employ renowned speakers in the rehabilitation field to talk about the latest technologies, treatments and protocols in this market and the attendees receive continuing education credit.

So, we have the highest level of service, therefore the most expensive products. This has been our strategy all along.

GROWTH OPPORTUNITIES

We believe that as the company grows, we will be the market and technological leader in rehabilitation of all kinds. Whether it's cardiac rehabilitation or physical rehabilitation for knees or backs, whether it's eyes or stroke recovery—it's an endless market.

Right now our specialty is physical therapy and orthopedics, and we are adding work evaluation equipment.

In the workplace, people aren't being screened, their jobs aren't set up to prevent injury and they're not trained to do the job properly to prevent injury. So, we are providing devices for pre-employment screening to test an injured worker's readiness to return to the job and to detect the progress of rehabilitation.

Because of our innovation and commitment to excellence we have earned several large accounts nationally. NASA, The Royal Air Force of Sweden and the United Kingdom and the British Olympic Committee are among our current customers.

"...spend the money on building your sales force and your service team and supporting them through tele-marketing, direct mail and videotapes."

EVERYONE GETS A PIECE OF THE ACTION

To ensure that our employees retain the motivation to provide the best service to our customers, we make sure the high performers are rewarded. It was always part of Malcolm's dream to share the company with the employees—particularly the first people hired because they took the biggest risk. He's been right in doing this. I know I wouldn't have joined the company without a promise of a return for my efforts. As a group, the employees now hold about twenty percent of the company's equity. This philosophy is coincidentally quite common in new California companies.

We treat our product managers differently than most other firms do. We believe our product managers provide the guiding light for the company. Tom Peters says it well when he calls them "product champions." And Loredan supports them as if they were champions.

These people wear a number of different hats. As the people in charge of in-house product demonstrations, they are our best salespeople. They earn a commission on each product they bring to market.

They must also convey customer specifications to the engineers. When a new product hits production, they are on the floor, putting the thing together and teaching the manufacturing folks how to use it.

Another important policy at Loredan is that all employees must earn their stripes. Nobody has seniority—it just doesn't mean much here. I don't care how long you've been here, if you don't keep your performance up, you don't belong here.

There is also no political positioning here. Your job security is based solely upon two things: commitment and performance. If someone is playing some kind of political positioning games, then we hired the wrong person and he or she doesn't stay here very long.

If we do make a hiring mistake, however, we assist the employee with the outplacement transition. We work with a great counselor who visits the leaving employee and helps him or her figure out where to go next.

If someone has to leave the company, I believe that everyone must share in the blame and in the burden of putting the pieces back together. I have heard stories about young successful companies leaving a trail of human wreckage in their wakes. I don't think this is fair. If there was a mistake, it was made in the hiring process. That is management's responsibility.

TAKE A SMALL BITE FIRST

Through the growth of our business, we have realized several key factors to our success.

First, you obviously need a good product.

Second, you must demonstrate that you can listen and act upon the request of the customer.

Third, I think you have to start small. I mean this in two ways. When starting out, you can't afford to make the all-encompassing product that suits everyone's needs. Make the product as simple as you can while giving the customer what he most often asks for. This will get to the market quicker with fewer mistakes. And start with a small sales territory. You can't take on the whole world from the get-go. Start in your own backyard and grow from there. Again, I agree with Tom Peters that you must become an international company, eventually. But your own geographical area is the point of least resistance for market entry.

ALWAYS BE A FUND-RAISER

I think cash management is also one of the most impor-tant issues—make sure you have cash and never think you can go out and raise the money when you have zero in the bank. A lot of people assume, "Well, I have another three months of money so maybe a month before I need money I'll go out and try to raise it." Always be in the money-raising mode. Take the money when you can get it.

GETTING THE WORD OUT

Of course, to continue growing, a company needs new customers. Direct mail is fairly inexpensive to do. Mail it out, then follow up. Also follow up on every lead that comes in.

Advertising is important also, but spend the money on building your sales force and your service team and supporting them through telemarketing, direct mail and videotapes.

A PUBLIC IMAGE OF THE FUTURE

Those are some of the principles we have used successfully as we head toward our goal—to go public by 1992. We are projecting the introduction of some new products that we believe will take our revenues to $25 million in 1990.

By 1992 we are striving for $50 million, at which time we plan to make our first public offering. Long-term, we believe that going public will enable us to raise the capital necessary to make us the $100 million dollar market leader that I know we can be!

Karen M. Comisso
Loredan Biomedical Inc.
1632 Da Vinci Court
P.O. Box 1154
Davis, CA 95617
Telephone: 916-758-3622
Telex: 7607445
Fax: 916-758-3493

Kathleen A. Cook

Kathleen Cook is founder and president of Computer Utilization, Inc., a computer training firm based in Rancho Cordova. She coordinates curriculum development and oversees all training services using her unique blend of expertise as an elementary school teacher and school administrator. Ms. Cook has a bachelor's degree in mathematics and a master's degree in educational administration from California State University, Sacramento.

I f you have ever sat in front of a computer screen with a manual in your lap, or spent hours wading through a series of confusing instructions that appear to have been written by an alien from Pluto, then you'll appreciate what Computer Utilization, Inc. (CUI) can do for you and your organization.

Computer Utilization offers computer training to small- and medium-sized businesses that want to increase profits through increased staff productivity.

As new computer technology proliferates throughout the business world, managers from the private and public sectors realize that professional training is the best way for their employees to learn such popular and practical programs as WordPerfect™, Lotus 123™, dBase™ and a host of others.

Rather than learning by trial and error, it is much more efficient and productive to gain computer knowledge in a structured training program.

Kathy Cook and her team offer hands-on instruction to federal and state agencies, school districts, and private companies such as Pacific Bell, SMUD, Blue Diamond Growers and others. Services include generalized computer training seminars, specialized training seminars, on-line computer training, curriculum development, needs assessment, management consulting services, project consulting, software package customizing and development, installation of accounting systems, support for DAC Easy™ and BRAVO™ accounting systems.

CUI occupies a facility near Bradshaw and Highway 50 that offers an optimum learning environment. Private training rooms, conference rooms and computer labs are furnished with ergonomically designed work stations and glare-free monitors. Students work on their own micro-computer units—complete with printer, color monitor and

"I switched it on and immediately black smoke started to billow out of the disk drive. I thought for sure I had ruined it."

"My goal was to create my own executive position, but I suppose I'm too independent as my creation ended up being my own business."

modems and are trained in state-of-the-art communications and electronic mail software. Hard drives are also available for each training unit. The equipment is IBM compatible and simulates actual business machines used in the Sacramento area.

Author's Note: *Computer phobia has no place at Kathy Cook's computer training facility. At CUI, the machine-like, high-tech environment is gently softened by a high-touch, friendly ambience that greets the newcomer and instantly puts them at ease. As they say, a business is merely an extension of its owner, and it is evident that Kathy has successfully extended her affable personality to Computer Utilization, Inc.*

When I was in high school I decided I wanted to be a teacher. After high school, I attended Sacramento State University and got my degree in math with a minor in education.

My first job was teaching the fifth grade. In my first class I had forty kids—thirty-five boys and five girls. At times it was crazy, but I loved teaching and I was good at it. The kids were great! I was able to communicate well and most importantly, they learned. I taught for many years and eventually became a principal on a temporary basis. I very much wanted to be a principal on a permanent basis; however, I wasn't able to find a position. That is the main reason I have my own business today. I feel that if I had received a principal position, I would probably still be principal.

DISAPPOINTMENT LEADS TO INNOVATION

When the opportunity to be a temporary principal came up, I was working on my thesis for my master's degree in administrative education. I wanted the position, so I put my education on the back burner. The position was given to me the day before school started. Nothing was ready. I was looking at a lot of preparation that had to be done literally overnight. After a lot of hard work, I wasn't able to obtain the promotion to permanent principalship that I wanted, and it was terribly disappointing.

I eventually finished my master's degree, but I found that it wasn't paying off. Soon after the temporary principal position ended, I implemented the first computer class in the district. That became my joy. It was fun to watch the kids get excited and turned on by this machine!

This was the beginning of my discovery that I had an interest in computers.

"Today we have well over one thousand different clients on the books."

PUTTING IT ALL TOGETHER

It took a year and a half from the time I began researching the computer program for the school in 1981 to the time that computers were actually being used in the classroom.

During that time I visited computer stores and knocked on many classroom doors in Sacramento. I eventually met Ted Perry, who is still in the San Juan School District, and the big guru around there for computers. He was a great help in getting the program started.

The computer arrived at my classroom door the day before Easter vacation. I had a few students load the boxes in my car, and I took the computer home to assemble. I had one week to figure this machine out. I didn't have a clue how to put these pieces together! That's how experienced I was; I expected it to arrive in one box—not nine.

After two hours the computer was assembled. I switched it on and immediately black smoke started to billow out of the disk drive. I thought for sure I had ruined it. The next day I returned to the computer store and found it to be an equipment problem. Thank goodness!

In one week, I had to prepare lesson plans of how I was going to let the kids use that computer and train myself to make it work. The students were waiting for me when I got to school at 7:00 a.m. on Monday. They learned how to use the computer faster than I expected, because they enjoyed working on it. Often, I'd have to throw my students out when it was time for me to go home!

"One big difference is we use teaching methods, where other people use training methods."

THE EYE-OPENING CONFERENCE

I worked with the computer classes for two years. During the second year, I helped teachers in the district learn how to use computers. I signed a part-time contract with the school, and my job was to move from school to school putting the computer programs into place within each school. I also served on a committee that helped Hewlett-Packard in Roseville set up programs for Placer County schools.

The Loomis School District sponsored a big conference for all the decision makers in Placer County. It was stimulated by Pacific Bell, Apple Computers and top computer people from Placer County. It was wonderful!

This conference lasted three days and had eight hundred people attending. Participating in this conference gave me the idea that I might be able to take on some consulting work. I knew I had some skills that I could share, but I also realized that I couldn't make a career of training teachers to use computers because the budgeting in the educational system can't be relied upon from year to year.

PERSPECTIVES ON SUCCESS FROM KATHLEEN COOK

- Provide quality
- Provide service with support
- Employ the best staff
- Encourage growth in all people
- Pay attention to your mission as a business
- Have fun helping people grow

GETTING ON TRACK

I wanted to do something different and I knew it had to be with computers. Consulting sounded more and more interesting, but I was still very limited in my computer skills. I decided to go to a career counseling firm, and I found that I was right on track.

More than anything else, the counseling program helped me to know myself. It gave me many different tools I could use, such as information interviewing, in which I talked to people about the jobs that were out there. My goal was to create my own executive position, but I suppose I'm too independent as my creation ended up being my own business.

THE INFORMATION INTERVIEW

I'm still not sure that I fit the definition of an entrepreneur, but I have come to realize through all of this that I am creative. I'm also competitive, and I feel that if something is right, I'm going to keep at it until it's working.

Having a sense of self helped me to be a good entrepreneur, but I gained that sense as I was out there kicking stones. I went to some of the contacts I had made at the conference and did some information interviews. I talked to Hewlett-Packard and to CableData. Some people seemed interested. The only problem I found was that I wasn't interested in being in their type of environment. So I decided to quit information interviewing and do some studies in education to be a computer consultant.

"Personal success for me is knowing that every day I'm going to be a better person than I was yesterday."

DON'T GIVE UP

Finally, I bought a computer and set up a little office in my home. There I started to help a few people learn how to use computers. I did this consulting for about six months.

Before long I decided that consulting wasn't going to work. I wasn't earning enough money. I was just about to quit when the telephone rang; it was the person from Pacific Bell who had helped put on the conference. He wanted me to go to Oakland to teach his employees computer literacy. I drove to Oakland the following week to check things out, but the whole way I was thinking, "What the heck am I doing?"

In Oakland he had two PCs and a team of forty people. I looked at the machine, and I realized that I didn't have a clue how to operate it. I took a manual home, managed to obtain access to an IBM computer (I had an Apple II), tutored myself on it and began teaching the class three weeks later.

GROWING INTO COMPUTER UTILIZATION

That was the start of my training business. My first time, I taught two classes for twenty people and they loved it! The next thing I knew there were ten more classes and then a unit of five hundred. All my clients were from Pacific Bell at that time. My training business just took off as I traveled between the four cities of Sacramento, San Francisco, Oakland and San Jose.

In 1983 the business was officially named Educational

"Financial success is looking at the bottom line and knowing that we had twenty-five percent growth this year."

Support Services. Demand increased. Travel became demanding and I decided to open my own training facility. It was time to incorporate. Today my business is called Computer Utilization, Inc.

Opening a facility gave me immediate status. It brought a professional image to the business, which started to bring other clients in the front door. We've diversified the client base with the addition of many private companies. We still have Pacific Bell, as well as Blue Diamond Growers, SMUD, and some fifty other firms. We also have forty to sixty state agencies with which we're proud to work.

Today we have well over one thousand different clients on the books. We train about five hundred people per month and a large percentage of our business is repeat.

We now do training in word processing, databases, spread sheets and DOS. We also do Pagemaker™ and Harvard Graphics. We are the only certified WordPerfect™ training center in the Sacramento Valley, and that has really helped raise our status.

NO CANNED PROGRAMS HERE

I think there are a lot of companies in Sacramento who do exactly what my company does, but none of them do it the way we do. Our strong point is that we care about the quality we put out and about what happens to the people who walk in the door.

Every class has a booklet that is written by us. It supports the presentation and assists in helping people learn from that presentation. Also, suggestions from previous students are incorporated into the material.

Our teaching methods are not training methods. The distinction is teaching lets the audience learn what they need to learn, while training doesn't necessarily take that into account. I have some good competitors out there who train, but the word training usually means that page-by-page, the student must do each of these exercises no matter what.

At CUI, we follow our course descriptions and our material, but we drop exercises or add new ones depending upon individual students' needs. It doesn't take much for us to modify a course agenda if we have a client who wants a specialized presentation, because we write our own material. This improves both the learning and the teaching.

THE ALTERNATIVE

Initially, my biggest stumbling block was my lack of self-confidence. As you go along, though, your confidence seems to build and now it isn't such an obstacle to me.

Every day there are problems I bump into along the road, various things I haven't planned for. If it becomes a dilemma, I immediately search for alternative solutions. There are always more solutions than problems. You just have to keep your eyes open for them.

SUCCESS CHANGES PEOPLE

My greatest reward is to have people say that our classes are the best they've ever attended. It's exciting to see that enthusiasm; it's one of the reasons I started in business. I'm a people person, and I want other people to be happy.

There's also the reward of knowing there will be a profit at the end of the month. "Everybody is paid and look what we did!"

We always do things as a team around here. That's really exciting, as it's fun to see people grow. One of my instructors is Erin. The Erin who started here and the Erin who teaches here now are two different people, she's grown so much. I look at my son, Ken, who is my accountant and a board member. He's also a different person from the experience of operating this business. My husband, Byron, who couldn't use a computer when I started, now teaches others that skill.

MANAGEMENT TRAINING

There are several people who have helped me along the way. One is my husband, because he was once my boss. When we first met, he was a superintendent and I was a teacher. He was the first to make the suggestion that I go for an administrative credential. At that time, there was no relationship between us, but he was the one who said I had the skill to do something more than what I was doing. He encouraged me all the way.

He taught me about paying attention to what other people are thinking and doing. I tend to get tunnel vision. I am task oriented and sometimes become so focused on where I'm going, I tend to forget what's

"...the rewards of building a successful business...I am finally the principal of my own school!"

happening with the other people. He's made me much more sensitive to my staff and has taught me a lot about managing.

My career counselor also was a great source of encouragement. He taught me the importance of writing things down. I wouldn't have defined my goals or described my business in writing if it hadn't been for his guidance. That is the very thing that makes you stick to where you think you want to go. I had done all of that so carefully that when it came time to take out our first loan for this facility, we were viewed as a model company. You wouldn't believe how fast that loan went through!

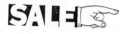

SELLING QUALITY

Personal success for me is knowing that every day I'm going to be a better person than I was yesterday. I'm going to use my mind on something new so it can grow. I'm going to give something of myself to somebody and not ask for anything in return.

Financial success is looking at the bottom line and knowing that we had twenty-five percent growth this year! There was a good profit in that. Everybody on my staff is receiving a good increase. We do things for people. All of that is important.

This business is successful because we have a quality product, as well as a quality staff. It was timed right and it meets a need. We have personal pride here and that's what makes a difference.

For people to succeed in a business like this, they have to know themselves well. They must make sure they really want to get themselves into all of this and that there's some financial security behind them to cover slow months. We had six months of expense money in savings before we started this facility. That's been our security.

PRINCIPAL AT LAST

Within the next three years we will have established at least one more center in Sacramento. We will be all over the state of California within the next ten years. How will our training have evolved by then? That's an unanswerable, but interesting, question. We'll have to wait and see.

For now, I am experiencing the rewards of building a successful business, not the least of which is that I am finally the principal of my own school!

Kathleen Cook
Computer Utilization, Inc.
Old Mills Winery Office Complex
9851 Horn Road, Suite 250
Sacramento, CA 95827
916-364-0203

Jim Floor
is the owner of one of the largest Amway distributorships in the world. His network extends to all fifty states and thirteen foreign countries. Prior to establishing his business enterprise, Mr. Floor was a lobbyist with Southern California Gas Company. He has a bachelor's degree in architectural engineering from Cal Poly, San Luis Obispo and a master's degree in business from Pepperdine University.

By now just about everyone in the world has heard of Amway, the grandfather of multi-level marketing that set the business world on its ear in the 1960s with a startling new concept for selling consumer products.

Starting with a line of soap products and now handling everything from attaché cases to credit cards, Amway has built a business empire by turning ordinary people with little or no business experience into entrepreneurs.

The concept is simple.

Distributors can make money two ways with their home-based business. They can buy the products at wholesale and sell them at retail for a profit, and they can sponsor others to do the same thing and receive a percentage of all products they sell.

As a distributor's organization increases—one Amway distributor signs up ten, who sign up ten, who sign up ten and so forth—the cash flow can grow to tremendous levels very quickly.

Jim Floor started with Amway about ten years ago. He estimates his annual income from his Amway business is well into six figures. He generates revenue as a "diamond direct"—one of the designations Amway uses to recognize its super-achievers—with Amway distributors in all fifty states and thirteen foreign countries.

He lives in an eight-thousand-square-foot home in prestigious Shelbourne Estates, drives a Ferrari, works when he chooses and basically lives the American dream.

The story of how he made it in Amway is truly inspirational, especially to those of us who saw the Amway opportunity, but failed, for one reason or another, to capitalize on it.

Is it still possible to make millions in Amway?

You bet it is!

"There's this idea in multilevel marketing that the only people who make money are people who come in at the ground floor."

"What Amway offers is

an opportunity for

somebody to develop

an extra $500 or even

$50,000 a month

depending upon his

needs."

Author's Note: *One of my own success secrets is to search for role models to emulate in my own quest for super achievement. In meeting and getting to know Jim Floor during our interview, I recognized in him that quality that a good mentor possesses: superior knowledge and the sincere desire to impart it to others who seek it. After our interview he showed me his storeroom of Amway products that he distributes through his extensive network of distributors. Thousands of cassette tapes take up one thirty-foot-long wall while hundreds of success books fill another large set of shelves—titles such as: Megatrends, Think & Grow Rich, The Real Race, How to Win Friends and Influence People, How to be Rich, Success— The Glenn Bland Method, Magic of Thinking Big, What To Say When You Talk to Yourself and others. Asked if he has read them all: Jim replied, "Absolutely!"*

There's this idea in multilevel marketing that the only people who make money are people who come in at the ground floor. Well, I like to say that we're at the ground floor right now.

I think back to 1959 when Amway was founded—those first ten to fifteen years were basement, not ground floor. In those days I think most people had a hard time building the business because they didn't have a consistent plan of action. It was trial and error, hit or miss. Also, Amway had only a small number of products and no real credibility in the marketplace.

Today there's a well-developed opportunity with Amway as a multi-billion-dollar corporation that is virtually debt free. We have thousands of products and hundreds of different suppliers networking with Amway, allowing each of us the opportunity to market those products, whether it's MCI long distance telephone service, Coca-Cola products or even automobiles.

Over the last thirty years the company has evolved from a backyard operation into a very large business. The projections by Stanford Research Center and Harvard Business School indicate that the 1990s will be the time when network marketing has a major impact on our economy.

Many people are concerned when they hear the words "network marketing" or "multi-level marketing" since it resembles a pyramid. It does have a pyramidal structure, but then, so does almost any business or corporation. However, unlike conventional businesses and illegal pyramids, there's a point where you develop independence from the person above you, which allows anyone to get to the top.

What Amway offers is an opportunity for somebody to develop an extra $500 or even $50,000 a month depending upon his or her needs. You can start out slowly and build it to a point where you are able to back off from your fulltime job if you desire and just do Amway.

"The beauty I found in the Amway business was that I could include my spiritual life in it."

KEEPING PRIORITIES IN LINE

I have always wanted to keep my spiritual life a very high priority. In fact, I believe it should be the number one priority in your life. I believe that there are five areas that should be prioritized. You should keep God first, your family second, the country you live in third, your job responsibilities or your profession fourth and the Amway business fifth. If you're going to be successful in the Amway business, don't cheat on those others to do it. You're not going to find happiness, and you won't be successful.

The beauty I found in the Amway business was that I could include my spiritual life in it. Previously, in so many business activities I almost had to play two lives. With Amway, I found that you could be the same person and still keep God first. I brought Him in as part of my business. Although I don't cram it down anybody's throat, I represent who I am without having to compromise.

In the corporate structure and the political arena, which are the two areas of my greatest experience, I had to look the other way and show up at times and places

"It seems to me that

the more naturally you

can present spiritual

life—reality of God—

the more accepting

people are."

even though I didn't want to be there.

PERSPECTIVES ON SUCCESS FROM JIM FLOOR
- Evolution of Amway
- A reality of God
- Lobbying the state government
- Amway provides the freedom
- Thick-skinned and soft-hearted
- Overcoming self doubts

ACHIEVING CONFIDENCE
The most rewarding aspect of the business has been the personal growth that I've gone through. It has given me a positive self-image and confidence. I know that I can do anything that I set my mind to. I can take on any project or take on any business opportunity, and if I keep my priorities straight, then I can accomplish what I set out to accomplish. I will do it.

CLIMBING THE CORPORATE LADDER
In 1967 I graduated with a degree in architectural engineering from Cal Poly, San Luis Obispo. We were in the middle of the Vietnam war at that time and there was an opportunity for me to take a draft-deferred job with Southern California Gas Company. I wasn't a war protester, but if there was an option besides firing an M-16, I was looking for it. I started at Southern California Gas Company as a field sales engineer, although it was more sales than engineering. I was a backup for any of the critical engineering positions with the utility.

For a total of sixteen years, I remained with that company, working my way up the corporate ladder. I became a supervisor and went on to middle management.

In 1976, I interviewed for the position of governmental affairs manager and became a registered lobbyist representing the Southern California Gas Company to the city and county of Los Angeles.

THE POLITICS OF POLITICS
The key to working effectively in the political arena is being able to anticipate potential dynamics or agendas that could affect you or the company you represent. It takes a lot of experience.

Gaining that experience means developing relationships and contacts with people so when there are rumors that something is going on behind the scenes, you receive a phone call. Sometimes someone will sneak up to you and say, "This didn't come from me, but...just so you know." The way in which you deal with that information is critical, too. It's like having undercover informants. You can't blow their cover and you can't act as though somebody gave you information. If you do, too often they'll know somebody's talking.

In 1980 I was transferred to Sacramento to lobby the State Legislature and Governor's Office. At that time my monthly Amway income was around $2,000 and was still a part-time thing. The gas company wanted me to quit the Amway business in order to take the promotion to the State Capitol, but I said "no." Large corporations—and the gas company was similar—often view something like the Amway business as a threat to their priorities. I refused to give it up. They finally agreed that it was all right as long as I kept it low-key. I never allowed a conflict of interest to occur.

I commuted to Sacramento from Los Angeles for a few months in the latter part of 1980, and moved the family up January 1, 1981. After getting settled in Sacramento I began building the business in this area, too, and now I have thousands of people in both locations. In fact, I have businesses in all fifty states and thirteen foreign countries.

CHOOSING A PATH TO WEALTH

There are basically three ways to make money. One is to trade hours for dollars, which is what most people do; another is to invest your dollars. The third is to invest in people either by employing, franchising or networking with them. If you trade hours for dollars, you can only increase your income two ways. First, to make your time more valuable or to trade more hours.

If you employ people, you have the added challenges of managing. If you franchise, there are some advantages such as those enjoyed by Ray Kroc with McDonald's. He can set up thousands and thousands of franchise operations and succeed as a result of putting people in business who are working hard to succeed.

In networking we don't have the upfront franchise cost or the limitation of having to go fulltime from day one. Someone can progress quickly or a little more slowly, but the point is the same because once you

"I drive a Ferrari, my wife drives a Jaguar. We live in a big home, and we go to Hawaii. We're normal people, but God is still first in our lives."

"Large corporations—

and the gas company

was similar—often

view something like

the Amway business as

a threat to their

priorities."

develop someone to a point of independence you'll receive residual income as a result of their success. This is where time freedom occurs as well.

FROM SIDELINE TO PROFESSION

I began with Amway in 1979 in Los Angeles, and within six months a small group of around fifteen people had developed in the network. It took quite a while just to build the foundation. Very little profit was realized at that point.

Within a year there were approximately a hundred people in the network. Instead of starting from a base of one we were now working from a base of fifteen, and we were netting out a profit of about $1,500 a month. I put in a year of part-time effort over and above my corporate position where I was making at that time close to $55,000 a year.

After eighteen months we reached the next level and then I was transferred to Sacramento with a raise to about $70,000 per year. I was lobbying on the state level and it took nine months to get back on the Amway track. We maintained what we had at that time with the business in Los Angeles and that meant lots of communication by phone. Once I began to develop the network in Sacramento the business grew rapidly. It was about twenty-four months from the time we moved to Sacramento until I left my lobbying career. Amway was now full-time with an income considerably larger than my corporate salary— actually, twice as large.

BUYING INTO THE SYSTEM

I think the key to my success was that I learned to set goals. I bought into the system, so to speak. In other words, I bought in emotionally, psychologically and mentally to the fact that Amway could give me my freedom. I knew that if I could follow a pattern of success that had been taught to me by people who were already living the way I wanted to live, that I could achieve the same success. I may have been somewhat naive, but again, that may have worked to my benefit. Sometimes when you're too sophisticated and you think things through too much, you can actually talk your way out of what is the best course of action for you. I think maybe I had faith not only in the Amway business and what I'd seen, but in what people were telling me. I duplicated as closely as I possibly could what I saw other people doing, mechanically applying those steps to the business. It began working for me.

LOOKING FOR OPPORTUNITY

One thing I have found is that you should never pressure anybody. I reached a point where I could talk anybody into joining Amway. They considered themselves dumb not to get into this great business, but I saw that I needed to back off and just concentrate on finding people who were *looking* for opportunity. I think that was critical to my success and the turning point of my business.

PROJECTING BELIEF

I believe in people. I believe in opportunity. I believe in myself. I began transferring those beliefs to my people. I told them that if I could do it, they could, too. When they didn't believe in themselves, I believed in them. I stayed in the books, I stayed in the tapes. I stayed with the functions, keeping myself on that level of belief that I could transfer on to them. I never became anybody's boss.

THICK-SKINNED AND SOFT-HEARTED

I think rejection is the toughest challenge anyone who has any sensitivity has to face. To care about helping people you must develop sensitivity to them. You must also develop a bit of insensitivity. When I got into this business I was very thin-skinned and hard-hearted. As I began to care for people and started helping other people succeed, I developed a thick skin and I became soft-hearted. I think most people are so thin-skinned that if anybody rejects or criticizes them it's a very difficult situation to handle.

Most people who criticize and ridicule are those who are struggling with their own self-image. I never had a highly successful person criticize me in the Amway business. I believe they felt good enough about who they were and what they were doing that I wasn't a threat to them.

A GIFT FROM GOD

I am convinced that the business was brought to me by God. It didn't happen by chance. It happened because the Lord knew I was seeking success and that I didn't want to sacrifice my spiritual life. Here, he presented a

"There are three ways to make money. One is to trade hours for dollars, which is what most people do; another is to invest your dollars. The third is to invest in people either by employing, franchising or networking with them."

"In networking we

don't have the upfront

franchise cost or the

limitation of having to

go fulltime from day

one."

package to me that said, "You can go out, become highly successful financially, be involved in other people's lives, and at the same time you can glorify me. You can put me first in your life and it doesn't have to be an either/or choice."

The most rewarding part of this from my perspective is that thousands of people have gotten their spiritual lives right as a result of the fact that I'm very open. They say, "Wait a minute, you have something I don't." It isn't necessary to go to them with a message. They come to me. People are very attracted because they feel they're missing out on something. God fills the void that everybody has in their life.

It seems to me that the more naturally you can present spiritual life—reality of God—the more accepting people are. I'm not some weird guy. I'm in the mainstream of life. I'm having a good time, enjoying nice things. I drive a Ferrari, my wife drives a Jaguar. We live in a big home, and we go to Hawaii. We're normal people, but God is still first in our lives.

The Amway business has been a great witnessing tool.

THE FUTURE

I plan to continue to work the Amway business as I do today—typically one or two meetings a week—until my kids are out of school and on their own. It has been nice living in an eight-thousand-square-foot home and having all the nice things that go along with that from the standpoint of raising a family, although I think that will change when the kids are gone. Once both of them are pretty much on their own, Margee and I see ourselves selling this home. Probably we'll buy three condominiums. We want to have one on Maui, one in this area somewhere or wherever the kids tend to settle, and one more in either Colorado or Park City, Utah. I would like to have one of those great big buses converted into a motorhome and have a driver anytime we want to travel throughout the United States. Someday I would like to write a book, and I have hundreds of books upstairs that I'd love to read.

ACTION CURES SELF-DOUBT

The biggest obstacle that I faced in building my business was overcoming self-doubt. That question that kept creeping in—am I kidding myself? Is this really going to come together for me?

Whenever I had thoughts like that, I increased my action, became busier. As I became busier, I concentrated on what I was doing. Those thoughts seemed to creep into my mind only when I wasn't productive. As long as I was putting effort in I was all right, as action seemed to overcome both doubt and fear.

I was the tall, skinny, awkward type of a kid all through junior high school. My mother was the most positive influence on my life when I was growing up. My dad, on the other hand, was a negative one, always calling me stupid and clumsy. I think you tuck those things away and they either become a motivation to prove someone wrong or an excuse for failure.

In some respects I think I'm happy it happened that way. Even though I felt horrible about myself and tried very hard in high school through athletics to prove my father wrong, he never once saw me compete. I fought hard and did everything I could and was somewhat successful there. I think when I started in the business world, and particularly in the Amway business, there was an underlying feeling that I couldn't have isolated back then. I couldn't have identified with it until maybe the last couple of years. I wanted to prove that I could do something really significant because of all those years he said I couldn't.

I look back now and I think that feeling was a major driving force. What's ironic is that now I provide virtually all of his financial support.

"I knew that if I could follow a pattern of success that had been taught to me by people who were already living the way I wanted to live, I could achieve the same success."

PAIN AND PLEASURE

I think we all go through a constant struggle in our lives, whether it's relationships, business, health or whatever. We struggle with these things called pain and pleasure. We're motivated to accomplish positive, pleasurable things in our life and we're motivated to avoid negative, painful things. We're always in a balancing act there. I think if we look back to see why we did or didn't do something at any certain time, it always has to do with motivation for gain or motivation to avoid loss. When we analyze the situation we'll find that the degree of motivation is why we did or didn't do something. Too often people don't build the Amway business or really succeed in their chosen profession because they concentrate on the negative or the hard work that's going to have to go into building, instead of concentrating on what they can gain. Personal growth and the growth that comes from stretching is painful, but it will result in your moving forward. True success is not what you have or what you do. True success is what you become. It's the secret of happiness. That's my basic philosophy and I think it applies to all areas of our lives.

Jim Floor
Floor Enterprises Inc.
7120 Summerwood Court
Loomis, CA 95650
916-791-4451

Alan Gold
*is a top producer for
The Acacia Group, the
oldest financial group
in Sacramento. Acacia
serves as an umbrella
for a variety of
financial services,
including banking, in-
vestments and insur-
ance. Mr. Gold came
into the insurance
business after a
successful career as an
archaeologist. He has
a bachelor's degree in
anthropology from Cal
State Northridge, a
master's degree from
UC Davis and has
written his dissertation
for a Ph.D.*

According to a Census Bureau survey, most people fail to accumulate enough money in their lifetimes to retire with dignity. In 1987, most Americans retired on less than $5,000 a year. Eighty-seven percent retired on less than $10,000 annually. Many of the people who make up these statistics have worked hard all their lives, just as you and I are working now.

"A portion of all you earn is yours to keep," says George Clason, author of *The Richest Man in Babylon,* a self-help book on achieving financial success.

The sad fact is that most people have too much month left at the end of their money. They don't have "extra income" to invest for the future—the present is tough enough. No doubt, in some cases, it's a matter of unlimited wants exceeding limited income, but most are desperately seeking ways to save money.

Alan Gold's self-proclaimed mission in life is to show people how to develop a painless, tailor-made system that will allow them to pay themselves first, which is the only way to guarantee long-term financial security.

A part of Gold's financial strategy includes life insurance.

He recalls how two of his first clients, a young married couple just starting out, benefited greatly from his counsel.

The man was an engineer and the woman was a homemaker. Gold listened to their concerns and created a strategy to accumulate money. Part of the estate plan was a $100,000 life insurance policy.

Two weeks after Gold took a deposit check, tragedy struck. The husband was killed in a car accident. A month later Gold was able to deliver a check for $100,000 to the family. It provided a way to maintain financial stability in the face of a personal disaster. Most important,

"If you look at the way in which archeology is conducted, it is quite similar to the way I currently conduct the insurance business."

"You guide them

through critical

passages in their lives

such as death,

financial crises,

sickness or accidents."

it was a legacy generated from the keen foresight of the provider.

Gold cites this incident as an extra dividend he receives from his line of work.

Author's Note: *Alan Gold looks like an insurance man—distinguished, slightly balding, self-assured, quick smile. His affable demeanor and inimitable low-key style are refreshing. His manner of speaking is soft, articulate, enunciating every "t" as he sifts through his memory banks for the exact words which communicate his thought with utmost clarity. Within this rather small man—a trim, five-foot-five—is a powerful force generating an aura of charisma that is truly inspirational to those who cross his path.*

I started out, oddly enough, in anthropology. I first got interested in this subject while in high school. They offered classes in archaeology at my school, James Monroe High School in the San Fernando Valley, and I went on to get my bachelor's degree in anthropology from Cal State Northridge, then my master's from UC Davis. After that, I wrote my dissertation for a Ph.D.

I was in archaeology for approximately fifteen years. I took it about as far as I could take it. I worked on sites in California, the Great Basin, the Desert West, the American Southwest, Mexico and the Near East, published books and articles and ran excavations. I even created several research centers, worked for the Bureau of Land Management, and the California Department of Transportation.

All I could have done further was become a teacher, a research scientist or a professional working for the federal, state or local government, all of which I had done. There was no place else I could logically take it. So I left the profession.

EXCAVATING THE INSURANCE BUSINESS
The transition to insurance wasn't as strange as it sounds.

When I was in archaeology I was essentially a people person. I wasn't really an academic. I did well in archaeology because I obtained most of my information from people rather than from books.

If you look at the way in which archaeology is conducted, it is exactly the same way that I currently conduct the insurance business. You go to a site, gather data by excavating in little squares, you screen the information, bag it, take it back to the laboratory, catalogue it, analyze it, put it on cards, run it through the computer, do some statistical analysis, some tests, develop a series of recommendations or reconstruct the past and then write a report.

That is exactly what I do now. I go to my clients' work/home (the site). I gather personal data—financial facts and feelings. Then this information is analyzed, many times with the aid of a computer, and the results are a series of recommendations and predictions for their financial future.

"I'm driven by numbers and I'm very persistent."

INSURANCE AS CRISIS MANAGEMENT

Insurance is much more rewarding than archaeology, however. You can make a very significant difference in a person's life by developing lifelong relationships, helping people protect their immediate financial security and helping them in times of need, sometimes tremendous need. I guide them through critical passages in their lives such as death, financial crises, sickness or accidents. We help them find ways to preserve their lifestyle in the future, in retirement and we deal with people in areas which are very sensitive, very emotional and very personal. That makes my job extremely rewarding.

INSURANCE MEDICINE MAN

I don't sell a product. I'm not a product peddler. What I do is work as a "needs driven" consultant and listen as a preventive medicine man to clues from individuals. These clues help me solve problems they have. I'm involved from the start to prevent financial calamities and to help them accomplish their financial objectives.

I guess what makes my particular style of doing business so different is that I provide a rich variety of value-added services. I want to be the financial man that my clients come to for many different services. In doing this we build a very tight, supportive relationship.

If they need to market their business, I'll suggest some ideas of how to achieve that. I'll help them through various strategies that I've developed. If they need a property or casualty insurance person, I'll have a referral for them.

INTERNAL PECKING ORDER

The internal anthropology of The Acacia Group is very interesting. There is a system whereby as you progress in production, you obtain more prestigious office space. When you first arrive, you get a little metal desk. As you reach certain levels of production, you then move to better office space.

In six months I went to the top, to the private office toward the front of the Acacia Headquarters Financial Center. In the first year I was number two in production in the office.

PERSPECTIVES ON SUCCESS FROM ALAN GOLD
- U. C. Davis
- People—the real wealth
- Value-added services
- A little metal desk
- Reverse helping relationships
- Study yourself

TIPS ON KEEPING SCORE

I'm driven by numbers and I'm very persistent. I developed a system early on whereby I track my progress—by hour, by day, by week, by month, by quarter. I monitor the number of phone calls I make, the number of people I reach, the number of appointments I've set, and the number of clients and sales I've created. I monitor everything closely and I do it all on a one-page form.

I also have worked out a scoring arrangement so I can give myself a score, and I know by that score on a daily basis whether I'm on track or not. For instance, if I make thirty phone calls I give myself four points. If I set an appointment I give myself one point. If I open a new case or conduct an actual interview—I call it a data collection—I give myself two points. If I close I give myself four points, and if I get a sale and create a client, I get another five points. Also, for every five recommendations or referrals, I give myself another point. My mission is to score one hundred points a week, or twenty points a day.

Based on that formula, by the end of 1990 I hope to be in the top five percent of all producers in the nation.

SYNERGY THROUGH GROUPS

Another important aspect of success is the formation of groups of similar-minded successful people to share ideas—to create a synergy.

To that end, I've worked with a certified public accountant and an attorney to develop an organization called The Y.E.S. group—Young Entrepreneurs of Sacramento. It's a business development organization, modeled after the book *Think & Grow Rich*. The Y.E.S. group brings unique professionals together to exchange business referrals. Additionally, it serves as a forum for guest speakers who are leaders in many different facets of their lives—be it economic, social, family, religious, civic, whatever.

I also belong to the Sacramento Jewish Federation, Jewish Breakfast Forum, The Small Business Network, the Sacramento Chamber of Commerce and the new Sacramento Club.

REVERSE HELPING

The concept of reverse helping is, as Zig Ziglar put it, simply that the more you do for others, the more they are going to do for you. It means doing without expectation of compensation. The Hebrew term is *tzedakah,* a righteous way of doing business. By developing reverse helping relationships, business becomes a stream. It comes back to you, like casting bread upon the water.

Still, you have to be selective in your giving.

If you give to people who are similar to you in their values, without the expectation of receiving, you're building into that relationship a bond, a trust, a respect that is unique. By building that, the scale is tipped so that some way in the future that balance—the principle of reciprocity—will come back, and you will always profit by it.

THE BIGGEST OBSTACLE TO SUCCESS: YOURSELF

No matter what anyone tells you, the biggest obstacle is always yourself. You have to develop certain personality traits and self-discipline. You need to tailor-make your business to you. Everyone's style is different; there are no easy formulas.

"If you give to people who are similar to you in their values, without the expectation of receiving, you're building into that relationship a bond, a trust, a respect that is unique."

"You can only be successful if you think successful."

If you come in here and observe the twenty different people who work in a similar capacity as I, you will find that they've all designed their marketplaces and the manner and style in which they run their businesses differently. It's a matter of searching through those techniques and strategies to find one that will work for you.

The biggest challenge is to be consistent and to communicate effectively to others and to yourself.

TALK TO YOURSELF

You can only be successful if you think successful. You have to start with yourself.

The key to communicating effectively with yourself is self-talk. Are you beating yourself up or are you giving yourself positive strokes? Are you identifying ways in which you can improve? Are you giving yourself credit for the challenges you've overcome? Are you eternally downplaying yourself, negating what you've accomplished and bringing that emotional level down?

GOLD'S SUCCESS GOALS

My life's purpose is to lead, inspire, guide, teach and motivate others to reach their goals of financial security and freedom as well as personal and professional excellence, and to accomplish this by word, deed and example. To make a difference, that's what Alan Gold's goal is, and everything I do fits into that.

For values, number one is family. It has to be family for me. I love my wife of eight years, Donna, and my three-year-old son, Jason.

Number two, of course, has to be health. If you're not healthy, you can't do anything else.

Number three for me is financial independence, so I monitor my income and savings and track my progress in that area.

Number four is tzedakah, or justice. Justice means I love others, I care about making the world a kinder, gentler, better, cleaner, more loving place for all mankind, and I love God. That's all it is, a righteous existence.

Number five is education—continuing and improving myself in education.

Number six is integrity—doing what I say I'm going to do; being what I am, honoring my commitments, living up to the highest standards, doing nothing that I feel in my gut is improper.

Number seven, which will probably be a challenge in my case, is humility—applauding the efforts of others, seeking ways to commend my associates, basically minimizing my own thing, not blowing my own horn so much.

PEOPLE ARE THE REWARD

My biggest reward is people. It's always the people. Meeting people and developing relationships with people. People are the wealth of the world. Dollars matter, but they come as a function of helping people and developing bonds, trust, relationships. That's what makes walking through the front door in the morning worthwhile.

"LET'S GET TOGETHER..."

My love for people translates into working tips, too. I have a key phrase I use over the phone with first-time clients. I say, "Let's get together. I don't know if I can be of any assistance or not, but the worst that can happen is that we'll become friends." The response has consistently been positive, because it's not just a line. That's really the way I feel, and the honesty comes through.

GOLD'S DEFINITION OF SUCCESS

Success is the progressive realization of predetermined, written, personal goals. That's the number one secret to my success. Study yourself. Set aside a period of intro-spection, go inside and study yourself. Sort it out, take it all in and ask yourself in your heart of hearts what it is that works for you and what doesn't. The answer will come. You'll have insight and it will click.

BASIC PRINCIPLES OF SUCCESS

It's all basic principles. The principles are the same in business as they are in religion. Love yourself, love others, be persistent, be consistent, help others, and give out greater service than you expect to receive. Do more either in the morning or at night. I have a period of planning and solitude where I set and prioritize my personal and professional goals for the day. I also do a weekly, monthly, quarterly and yearly review of the larger goals. I set up written statements of my values. I take those values and then in turn change them into either

"Let's get together. I don't know if I can be of any assistance or not, but the worst that can happen is that we'll become friends."

long-range or short-term goals. I actually put action steps down, set target dates and integrate those target dates into my daily activities. It is a whole system, a way of life.

LOVE WHAT YOU DO

Another key, maybe the ultimate key to success, is to find something you love so much that you would pay to do it, and do it with all that's in you. You will be very successful at it. The key is finding something you have a passion for.

Alan Gold
The Acacia Group
2710 Gateway Oaks Dr., North
Suite 105
Sacramento, CA 95833
916-920-5695

E. William Henriod,
C.P.A. owns and
operates Complete
Business and Tax
Service. He was
formerly with Peat,
Marwick, Mitchell &
Co. and was a partner
in two CPA firms prior
to starting his own
firm. Mr. Henriod
majored in accounting
at Golden Gate Uni-
versity. He has served
on the Board of
Directors of the
Sacramento Chapter of
the California Society
of CPAs. Additionally,
he has served on the
Taxation and Person-
nel Committees of the
state society.

E. William Henriod was born in Lowell, Massachusetts, fifty-three years ago and has been in the public accounting arena since 1959. Three important relationships in Bill's life define who he is, and why he is so successful.

The first is his family. Bill has been married for over twenty-six years to Sharon Forsell—his best friend and adviser. Sharon is a master teacher with over twenty years of experience. The couple have four children: Therese, Erika, Joel and Melanie.

The second important relationship is the one Bill develops with his clients. He believes in taking the time to earn his clients' trust, and to become an integral part of their businesses.

Bill's involvement with his church rounds out his life and his accomplishments. Professionally, Bill has the diversified expertise of membership in a Big Eight accounting firm, two partnerships and a franchise. He has a thriving business—Complete Business and Tax Service, which he started in 1981. The goal of his new venture is to provide effective management tools to owners and managers of small and medium-sized businesses.

Bill's ability to expand beyond mere number crunching has resulted in a solid, loyal client base, as well as a realistic goal of doubling his business in the 1990s.

"I am not limited to earning what others earn, nor should I gauge my performance against that of others."

Author's Note: *Bill was the first person selected to be in Success Secrets of Sacramento's Business Professionals. We were introduced through a mutual friend who highly recommended that I talk with Bill about his successful business philoso-*

"These are the things which give me extraordinary satisfaction—family relationships, church service and client service."

phy. It turned out to be an excellent introduction. Upon our meeting, Bill befriended me in minutes with his non-stop humor and optimistic attitude. In this chapter he reveals how his deep-seated values have helped him succeed not only in business, but in life.

Years ago when I worked for the accounting firm of Peat, Marwick, Mitchell & Co., I found that the partners of the firm earned thirty to fifty thousand dollars a year. Before my father died in 1951 he never made more than thirty-five thousand dollars annually as a landscape architect. For years I unconsciously felt that it would be wrong for me to earn more, so I didn't.

I have since learned that I am not limited to earning what others earn, nor should I gauge my performance against that of others. Each of us is unique. We must not allow false concepts to limit our potential.

I have also found that if I will help others reach their goals, it is inevitable that I will gain mine. In the selling situation, I have come to realize that if I am interested in adding a client for monetary reasons, rather than to help with the prospective client's problems and needs, that client may seek services elsewhere.

I firmly believe that in the initial stages of selling my services, prospects can sense insincerity, making them wary of my ability to provide what they need.

THE JOYS OF LIFE

I started my own practice in mid-1981, as part of a franchise, with no clients and with very few leads for prospective clients. My original internal business goal was to have about fifty monthly clients and show an annual net profit of around eighty thousand dollars.

Also, since I am actively involved with my church and family, I wanted to have ample time to devote to each. I am proud to say that I have reached those initial goals.

In 1988, I left the franchise to give it a go on my own. I am now earning a substantial annual income, a figure consistent with many professional service firms. I take four, full-week vacations with my family and I am able to attend most of my children's extracurricular events. I am also able to participate in midweek church activities.

These are the things which give me extraordinary satisfaction—family relationships, church service and client service.

CONTROLLING DESTINY

Even though I had been a partner in two CPA firms, I never felt that I was self-employed before. I did not have control over my time or destiny. One reason was that my ownership in these firms was not a controlling one— always less than fifty percent.

I broke out on my own because I sought independence and flexibility. Since I am in business to serve my clients, I knew I would also have to accommodate their needs.

There have been times of postponed vacations, and I have spent unusually long hours in meeting the needs of my clients. Whatever accommodations I might make, they are never allowed to encroach upon professional judgments and personal values.

IMPORTANT PEDIGREES

One of the reasons my business is so successful is my background and extensive training in the field. I attended Golden Gate University in 1964 and passed the CPA exam on the first attempt—which only five percent of accounting graduates are able to do.

It is very important to belong to professional organizations, and I have served on the Board of Directors of the Sacramento Chapter of the California Society of CPAs. Additionally, I've served on the Taxation and Personnel Committees of the state society, as well as retaining membership in several other local, state and national organizations.

To gain corporate experience, I worked in the tax department of Peat, Marwick, Mitchell & Co.—one of the original Big Eight—and the regional firm of John F. Forbes.

Having practiced accounting in the Sacramento area for over seventeen years, either as a partner or on my own, I believe I have a firm sense of the community and its needs.

"People forget how fast you did a job, but they remember how well you did it."

"Our function is to be

our clients' 'strong

right arm' and to

provide support to

them in the decision

making process."

THE FRANCHISE AS EDUCATIONAL TOOL

When I discontinued my franchise association, I changed the name of my Dixon-based business to Complete Business & Tax Services. The original reason I had for choosing the franchise route was to gain skills in marketing, since accounting curriculum and partnership experience did not deliver this essential ability.

Although I have ended the franchise relationship, I still maintain close ties with other members of the group. In fact, we recently presented a two-and-one-half-day seminar in San Francisco for the National Association of Computerized Accountants.

PERSPECTIVES ON SUCCESS FROM BILL HENRIOD
- Seeking independence
- Professional alliances
- Not speed, but accuracy
- Strong right arm
- Subliminal selling skills
- Helping others to succeed

EFFICIENT QUALITY

My business operates with one bookkeeper, one part-time utility staff member and myself. Maximum use of automation and an in-house computer system allows very rapid, accurate processing of our clients' accounting data.

However, we bear in mind what Howard W. Newton said: "People forget how fast you did a job, but they remember how well you did it." We furnish our clients with a system that provides ways to save time and money in processing accounting data. Use of the system's simple forms allows us to process information quickly and efficiently.

Each month, every accounting client receives a balance sheet, operating statement, all journals, employee payroll records and a bank reconciliation. Some clients receive cash flow statements and comparative statements. These are the essential tools needed by our clients to effectively manage their business and control their costs.

In most situations, we furnish clients with consultations at no additional cost, as we sincerely want our customers to discuss their business matters with us. I have learned from experience that the clients will not contact us as often as they should if they think they will be charged for every telephone call.

Our function is to be our clients' "strong right arm," and to provide support to them in the decision-making process. We realize that we can succeed only if our clients succeed; therefore, we will do all we can to aid them in being successful. This emphasis is one way of practicing "win-win" philosophy.

MEETING EXPECTATIONS

Accounting and taxation are people-oriented businesses, people dealing with needs of other people. A business must have a good staff to serve its customers adequately. My practice is operated on the principle that people will perform as we expect them to perform, and as we communicate those expectations to them.

With this expectation comes the responsibility and authority to direct their own actions and time. Flexibility is a benchmark of my personnel policies. While I desire reasonable office hours to be maintained, my staff members are free to adjust their hours to meet their personal needs.

The overriding limitation is that quality and timely services to our clients must be maintained. I have been blessed with a conscientious staff—people who care about the success of our clients and of our business. My employees consistently produce high-quality service for our clients, and I sincerely appreciate them. One should not take employees for granted. There is a sign in our office that says, "The only way to avoid mistakes is to gain experience. The only way to gain experience is to make mistakes." Isn't that true?

When an employee of ours makes a mistake, we use it as a teaching opportunity to show what was wrong, and what is the correct way to handle the problem. The individual's ego remains intact, since we have attacked the problem and not the person. We are assisting the employee to grow and develop, which, I believe, is our responsibility as employers.

REFERRING TO PROMOTION

To promote the business, we have tried most marketing techniques. We have tried cold calls, warm calls and direct mail. We have used telemarketing, advertised in newspapers, television, magazines and in anti-drug campaign materials. We have sought referrals. Newspaper ads work for us during tax season. TV advertising has not

"The only way to avoid mistakes is to gain experience. The only way to gain experience is to make mistakes."

"I know now that most fears are unfounded because we fear what we do not know and understand."

been too successful; however, we are considering cable TV advertising on CNN or ESPN, since we have already produced a videotape.

The main path of growth has been from referrals by our clients. While clients will often recommend other clients to us without encouragement, we have found that a referral program is most effective. We ask for referrals from our clients, and by doing this, we honor our clients by showing we appreciate them and their judgment. No client has ever refused to furnish a referral!

MASTERMINDS

Selling geniuses have helped our marketing strategy also. Tom Hopkin's course, *How to Master the Art of Selling Anything,* and Zig Ziglar's book, *Secrets of Closing the Sale,* are two resources which can turn anyone into an effective salesperson. A verse in scripture says, "If ye are prepared, ye shall not fear." These sources helped me to become prepared, and to control the fear—the fear of meeting new people, fear of rejection, fear of failure and fear of the unknown.

WHITE WATER THRILLS

As I have grown older, I have tried to face my fears and control them. For example, I recently went on a white water rafting trip down the upper reaches of the American River. It was a heart-pounding event, and there were more than a few moments when I had doubts about my sanity in going on this excursion. The trip was exhilarating, wet, wild and wonderful. I made two runs that day, and I am looking forward to going again soon.

I know now that most fears are unfounded because we fear what we do not know and understand. I think I may learn about mountain climbing and try a little of it some time in the future—even though the thought of clinging tenuously to the face of a rock, hundreds of feet above the ground, makes me uncomfortable.

With knowledge and training, I know I can control these fears also. If I can do it on the American River, then there is no reason why I can't do it climbing mountains, making presentations, fighting the IRS or other potentially scary situations in life. Somewhere I read that if we have healthy minds, we are the sole limiters to the realization of our talents. Even those with physical handicaps can accomplish amazing feats.

Recently, a mountain climber who had lost the use of his lower body in a climbing accident successfully climbed El Capitan, in Yosemite National Park. El Capitan is a granite, vertical monolith that rises about thirty-eight hundred feet from the valley floor. It took him almost a week to complete the climb. It is obvious he thought he could do it and he did, using just his arms!

A CHALLENGING FUTURE

My goals are changing as my business and children mature. A short while ago my son, now a sophomore in high school, told me that he wanted to come into my business. That had to be one of the happiest days of my life. In my wildest dreams I had never dared hope for such an association with him.

To support two families, I will need to double or triple the size of the practice. This increased business will also provide a platform from which he can launch further firm growth, as his dream is to have many office locations. My work is cut out for me. I will need to produce twice the growth in the next decade as I have in the last.

MIRRORS OF TRUST

One of the most important factors in my business and personal life is that I create a feeling of trust with other people. I use a very successful technique to achieve this faith, which I learned from *Subliminal Selling Skills,* by Dr. Kerry Johnson.

This method is known as "mirroring." It is simply doing what the other person is doing. People respond to people who are like them—those who move, talk and think like them. For example, I had a meeting once with a man named Sam, who had been referred to me by one of my clients.

When I met Sam, his reaction to me was very cool. He appeared apathetic about our meeting. His body language showed he was closed to open communication. He crossed his arms and legs and leaned back in his chair, and turned it to an angle so he wasn't directly facing me. His voice was low, slow and lacked excitement of any kind.

I decided to follow his lead, and so I did what he did, only I left my chair squarely facing him. I crossed my arms, sat back in the chair, crossed my legs, and tried to mirror his speech style. I began my presentation and in

"One of the most important factors in my business and personal life is that I create a feeling of trust with other people."

"Warm relationships

are a reward in

themselves."

less than a minute, he uncrossed his legs. Several seconds later I did the same. The presentation continued. He responded to a question, and his speech showed more interest and animation. He uncrossed his arms, as my speech followed the increased pitch and tempo he had displayed. I uncrossed my arms to follow his lead several seconds later. I pointed out something in the presentation to him and he leaned forward. I immediately did the same.

At this point his voice began to show normal animation, so I followed suit. Then I passed him. I picked up the tempo and excitement in my voice. He now became more animated in his body movements. Finally, we had developed rapport! I decided to test that rapport, so I leaned back in the chair. He did the same.

Sam and I had developed trust between us. Why? Partially because I was like him. I did what he did and spoke the way he spoke. Additionally, I observed that he was a visual person, meaning that he used words such as "see," "view," "perspective" and "clear." He thought in pictures, that is, visually. I too used visual words, and showed him what our service would be like, and it worked!

WORDS TO THE WISE

Warm relationships are a reward in themselves. Success in life, in business, at home, etc., can be measured by the success we have in working with others to help them realize their greatest potential. When helping others to succeed, we will do likewise.

A wise saying goes, "People rarely succeed at anything unless they have fun doing it." Enjoy your business. Enjoy your clients or customers. Enjoy your employees, and help them to enjoy their work. Enjoy your family. Enjoy life. What could be more fun? What could be more successful?

E. William Henriod, C.P.A.
Complete Business and Tax Services
1170 N. Lincoln, Suite 101
Dixon, CA 95620-2119
916-678-1648

Craig Johnson
is owner of The Image Works, one of Sacramento's premier graphic design firms. He received his formal training from the California College of Arts and Crafts in Oakland and the Colorado Institute of Art in Denver. Mr. Johnson has won many regional and national awards for his graphic design.

With more than one hundred graphic design studios, Sacramento is recognized as one of America's largest centers of graphic design. Many local designers are regularly featured in trade publications and serve as guest speakers at seminars and conferences across the nation.

Our overcommunicated society is spawning the need for these creative artists, who can communicate a message effectively in brochures, direct mail, advertisements, and billboards.

As Richard Wurman states so aptly in his book, *Information Anxiety*, "As the only means we have of comprehending information is through words, numbers and pictures, the two professions that primarily determine how we receive it are writing and graphic design...yet the orientation and training in both fields are more preoccupied with stylistic and aesthetic concerns...rather than making graphics comprehensible."

This statement may be disconcerting to award-winning designers, but to Craig Johnson—who has also won his fair share of first place design awards—the needs of his clients come first.

Clear communication and an image that is custom fitted to each client's marketing objectives and style of doing business are Johnson's primary considerations in approaching a project. That, coupled with his talent and ability to deliver understandable graphics, makes Johnson one of the most sought after designers in Sacramento.

To him, a picture truly is worth a thousand words, but only if it communicates the intended message clearly and quickly.

"I've learned that getting where you want to be is a simple process. Identify points A and B, then the best way to get there is a straight line."

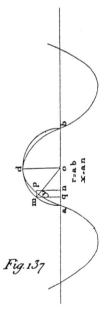

Fig. 137

"I had the basic foundations of design knowledge, but it was solving project and client problems that really put the chrome on the hubcaps."

Author's Note: *Craig Johnson's design studio resembles the inside of the Starship Enterprise. Rounded partitions and sterile white workstations combine to create an aura of intrigue and artistic charm. When Craig talks about graphic design, he's effervescent—like a bottle of soda that has been shook up and is ready to explode. His employees and associates say his enthusiam is infectious and that "it's impossible to be down when C. J. is around."*

I have bad eyesight and didn't get glasses until my junior year of high school. For years I could not see the chalkboard, and because of that, I was labeled the class clown and put in the rear of the room—which further affected my ability to see.

It was apparent that I wasn't going to make it in academics, but fortunately I became interested in crafts and that's where I started excelling. I would bring a big wad of molding clay to school and in class I would make things inside my desk. I would take paper clips and bend them to make little cars and motorcycles. I had a whole world under my desk. It was almost like artistic braille.

My senior year in high school I met a friend of my brother, who turned me on to graphic design. He told me how he designed brochures, logos and ads and had fun doing it. He also told me that it was a great business to be in—you make a lot of money, meet crazy people and have a good time. I thought, hmm, that fits my criteria perfectly.

Halfway through my senior year I started building a small portfolio. I pulled some of my art projects and did what I could with those, and finally I was accepted by an art school.

TAKE IT ONE STEP AT A TIME

I've learned that getting where you want to be is a simple process. Identify points A and B, then the best way to get there is a straight line. You yourself determine what point

A and point B are. Common sense tells me if you want something you have to approach it one step at a time. I start out with what I want and then I backtrack, just the way I do a lot of design work. After determining what the client wants to do, I backtrack to find out where I want to begin. Then I break down each different step and evaluate it to determine the shortest path to the end of the road. That's the goal.

"My biggest success comes when I've given a person what I felt was good for him."

LIFE IN A PINSTRIPE SUIT

Like most artists, I have a strong independent streak in me, and during my first few years in the design business I found it hard to deal with people in business suits. I was this mountain boy who wanted nothing to do with that type of lifestyle. Years later I came to realize you have to accept the pinstripe suit to get to first base. If you want to make good money you have to go to that kind of ball-park and play their ballgame.

NO PROBLEMS: ONLY SOLUTIONS

Some designers tend to fall apart when given a problem by a client, and they can't operate. An old associate of mine taught me to find the solution inside the problem, to view the latter as an asset rather than a negative. For instance, if you sit down at the drawing board, faced with a difficult problem and you let it be a negative, you're not going to be able to see past it. It will be a brick wall that you keep running up against. The trick is to make a ladder to get over it, and then the problem becomes the solution.

Of course, finding the solution within the problem can be very hard. I would go home many times after working ten to twelve hours to hit the reference books and magazines. I searched the pages for that solution. What made this ad or that brochure work? The answer was undoubtedly there somewhere. It had to be.

I committed myself to finding these answers. I had the basic foundations of design knowledge, but it was solving project and client problems that really put the chrome on the hubcaps.

STARTING OUT IN SACRAMENTO

When I first started in Sacramento I worked out of my house, doing anything that came along. I'd paint a truck if I had to! I already had a potential client pool because I

"My feeling has always been that if a job gives you satisfaction the money is going to come along with it. If people were to concentrate strictly on making money, there would be a bunch of greedy people out there and I'm not willing to contribute to that."

had worked previously with other people in town, and I spent a lot of time on sales. In three months I contacted over four hundred people, and ended up with $65,000 worth of contracts in that short amount of time. Again, point A to point B. I found out who I wanted to work for and took them on one at a time.

From previous jobs I had collected such paperwork as purchase orders and other billing aspects of the business. I brought these along with me. So by retaining the record-keeping information that successful people had taught me, I knew what I had to do to make it in starting my own business. I knew also it took a lot of hard work.

MATCHING GUCCI STYLE WITH GUCCI DESIGNS

I think what makes The Image Works hum is me, my ability to see things without having to have a pad of paper in front of me, to be able to read somebody. For example, I look at someone and see that they're wearing navy blue pants and Gucci shoes. I shouldn't give them a brown letterhead. Instead I should give them a blue letterhead, and it should have an affluent style. I try to match the client's style as best I can.

Not everybody has that ability. They take their own design style and say, "I really like this type of style," or "I really like this paper stock today so that's what I want to use for my next design project."

I don't do that. I take colors, design, and ideas and make them fit with the client's needs. As I said before, I backtrack. What does this client need and what's going to make his product or service sell? I try to match the design with the style. If she has a country style then I may give her a country style image. My biggest success comes when I've given a person what I felt was good for them. They pay the bills, therefore they get what they want, but a key ingredient is having common sense and being able to read people's tastes correctly.

PERSPECTIVES ON SUCCESS FROM CRAIG JOHNSON
- The nearsighted artist
- Point A to point B
- $65,000 worth of contracts
- Design and image
- Angels and devils
- Subliminal messages

ODD NUMBERS HELP

I categorize all my work and break it down into three simple things. Odd numbers have always worked for me. I feel that when you have one item you can focus on that item alone, but if you have two items it's like a ricochet—you go back and forth. When you have three items there seems to be harmony. It's something like the three-legged stool, well balanced. That's why I break design down into three elements: words, color and image.

HAPPINESS BEFORE MONEY

To me the money is not as important as being happy with what I do. I could gross $250,000 or $500,000, and that wouldn't be any problem. It may just cause me to die at thirty-five and not have much to say about it. I wouldn't be around to spend the money.

First on my list of priorities is quality design work. I want to create something that I'm happy with and that my clients are happy with. The fact that I make a million dollars doing it is not an important factor. The money will be there.

You not only go into business to make money, but also to make yourself happy and contribute to the community. My feeling has always been that if a job gives you satisfaction the money is going to come along with it. If people were to concentrate strictly on making money there would be a bunch of greedy people out there and I'm not willing to contribute to that.

ESTABLISHING A BUSINESS IMAGE

Graphic design is becoming more and more important in today's business world since our society is built heavily on phone and mail contacts. The image of the business is seen by people before they ever meet the person behind it. For this reason it's important for a business to have a good design. Your first impact on a business person is not when you walk in the door, but when he sees the name Craig Johnson from The Image Works on the message from his secretary.

The company name, The Image Works, is my first contact with any potential client. People need to have an established visual image of what somebody is before they ever meet them. They must have an idea that this person is professional before they ever meet him because of the amount of competition out there.

"I probably glow in the dark sometimes because a job turned out so nice and I'm so happy."

"The fact that I made

a quarter of a million

dollars one year

doesn't turn my light

on, because again,

money is not the

immediate goal."

THE LOGO: A PERSONAL CORPORATE STATEMENT

A logo is the image of a company, and this is what people see first. When I design a logo, I ask my client first about the company style. It could be traditional, contemporary, corporate or conventional. Their answers tell me how this client or this company would like to be perceived by its customers.

To get a clear idea of what is wanted in a logo, the person and company need to know what they're trying to accomplish, not what kind of logo they think they need. The next step is to devise some approach to accomplish those goals. I then do my best to set that desire into the graphics.

YOUTH—AN OBSTACLE?

The biggest obstacle someone in this business faces is experience. In my case, it was other people's perception of my lack of experience. Since I'm young, people don't accept me immediately as they would an older person, who they may feel will understand their needs better. They come into The Image Works design studio and they're putting their whole business on the line with this person who looks like one of their kids. In that situation, being young can pose a problem.

I've even gone to the extent of having gray put in my hair by a stylist just before a meeting with a very important client. I'm serious. I went in to get gray stripes on the side because I wanted to go in there and really knock them out. I knew that I had the background, the portfolio and the right graphics, but when I looked in the mirror I felt I had to make myself look older. Unfortunately, the color wouldn't hold in my hair.

THE REWARD IS THE WORK

The greatest reward is a happy client. When someone tells you that you did some really good work you feel great. It's wonderful to know you took their design problem and created something out of nothing. You put all this magic and sparkle into it and the lightning bolt comes down and blesses you and there it is. There's the idea—it's perfect. It's laid out, the rough sketch set up, and they love it.

When you hand over that final printed piece and you know it's hot, it's a supercharge. There's just nothing like it! I probably glow in the dark sometimes because a job turned out so nice and I'm so happy. Sometimes I make a profit and sometimes I don't, but that's not what matters. The money isn't the motivating factor. Happiness comes from my client's appreciation of a job well done.

The fact that I made a quarter of a million dollars one year doesn't turn my light on, because again, money is not the immediate goal. After I get to point B, point C might be the pot of gold. I don't think you can plan entirely for point C. You just do your best work and eventually you'll get there.

"I think success is happiness. I think it's feeling as though you've done something good for somebody."

DEFINITION OF SUCCESS

Success for me is not defined by money alone. I know a lot of wealthy people out there and they're not entirely happy. I think success is happiness. I think it's feeling as though you've done something good for somebody. It's the old hometown boy in me that goes back to when I used to mow a lawn for a little, old lady. When I was finished mowing I would rake all of the leaves into a neat pile. The most satisfaction I got from that was her coming out and saying, "Boy, that's a nice lookin' job."

The important part is the pat on the back. It's important to have somebody appreciate your hard work. You love getting the money, but it's knowing you did something good for somebody that really makes you happy.

DRIVE —THE NUMBER ONE SUCCESS SECRET

My only real secret for success, if you can call it a secret, is my drive. In the five years since I started this business I've probably put in ten years' worth of labor. There've been a lot of late nights. It's basically drive. It's starting at point A and reaching the goal, point B.

Drive has also been the reason behind some of my failures. I've lost a lot of time in my life when I could have been with my family or old friends. I could have done a lot of different things with the time I've spent making The Image Works something to be proud of. When I look back on it at some time in the future I think I'm going to feel very happy about what I've done and wouldn't change a thing.

When I hear people say "everything in moderation," I laugh because I don't do anything in moderation. I give one hundred and fifty percent on everything I do or give nothing at all.

"When I hear people say 'everything in moderation,' I laugh because I don't do anything in moderation. I give one hundred and fifty percent on everything I do or give nothing at all."

FIRM GOALS, NOT LONG HOURS

Long hours aren't necessarily the key to success though. The right goals need to be set. It's exactly like a design project: the way to succeed is to sit down and examine what you want to achieve. You plan where you want to be in one year and where it is you want to be in five years and so on. This is a critical step.

I sat down with a business planner when I first started my business. She had worked with other design firms who wanted to purchase their own buildings, and she normally set them up on a five-year plan for that. I said I wanted to do it in three years, and she told me I was crazy. I said, "Of course I am, but I want to do it in three," and I did.

The goals you set need to be ambitious—that's what drives you.

I put tremendous pressure on myself to do something. I have a way of procrastinating in order to build pressure to perform. I'm not a slow person. I like to make decisions and to move and make things happen fast. I don't like to wait.

BALANCING WORK AND LIFE

You can get carried away with the drive. I think my major goal, now that I'm to the point where I've had some success, is to just enjoy it. I've taken more of a backseat, not working as hard as before. I want to enjoy what I've created for myself. I want to travel and get my life back in order, maybe be a little more human again. I've been a robot for far too long.

ADVICE FOR OTHER ENTREPRENEURS

The first important step, though it sounds obvious, is to find out what you want to do. Are you in a business that you enjoy? Are you selling cars but would prefer to be selling computers or real estate? Again, establish a basis for what makes you happy. Don't use money as the primary factor. If you put money in the first slot you're sure to be a loser. There's a bit of an evaluation that has to be done. Where have you been, what did you do wrong and what do you want to be?

As they say, you are what you eat. If you don't evaluate your feelings you could be headed for disaster. Your business fails because of who you attract. If you are doing work for bad clients it's because they are the only ones you talk to. Your business and your life are reflections of yourself.

"The goals you set need to be ambitious, that's what drives you."

THE HARP AND THE PITCHFORK

I have two little people—one on each shoulder—that I use as advisers. I've got a "devil" on one and on the other I have an "angel." The devil can talk much louder than the angel, but the angel is the main man as far as advice goes. He says to go for it, that you can do it. It's good advice. The angel is the quieter one, and it's taken me many years to learn to listen for his advice.

If you're faced with a problem, the devil can sell you anything. "That car looks great" or "I bet you'd look cool in that car." The angel quietly says, "Don't buy the car." You have to listen because that's part of where the balance is. There needs to be a balance between what you feel is right and wrong. If your ethics are in the right place then your thoughts will be also. When you're doing something for the right reason you will be successful in anything you tackle.

GOOD AND BAD CLIENTS

The most challenging clients are people who don't know what they want. They don't know where they want to be and I have to help them come up with a plan. They're not sure of themselves and therefore not sure that what I've given them will work. Their indecisiveness makes them difficult to work with.

The opposite extreme is someone who is overly decisive: "This is what I want, and this is how you should do it." Even if you know the ad is not going to work for him, he won't take your advice. There are many people like that and the only choice they've given me is to give them what they want.

The good clients are people who say, "Why don't I want an ad?" I tell them that it's because what they're selling or their service is something that is not applicable to advertising. I might tell them it's more applicable to a brochure or to a direct mail piece. They say, "Really, why is that?" I tell them that this way they can target their market, get specific, and it's cost effective. An ad gets read in two seconds, while a direct mail piece may get read in five to eight seconds.

Good clients are willing to listen. They make solid business decisions based on other peoples' expertise. I've

"The first important

step, though it sounds

obvious, is to find out

what you want to do."

been designing for over ten years and I know when the color green is going to work and when the color red isn't, but if the guy loves red and that's all he's willing to use, I'll give him a red brochure. I just won't feel his loss because he wouldn't use my strengths to help him succeed.

TIPS FOR A NEW BUSINESS

I think it's very important for a new business to start out with its own stationery package and logo. You go through a task of selling a service or product, and in doing this you have to send a prospect a letter, support material or whatever. If you have a poorly designed letterhead on bright orange paper then all the client will see is this bright orange paper. He will not read it.

On the other hand, if you have a nice, pleasing letterhead, it will be read. It's almost like a subliminal message. The customer looks at the colors and the idea, and if all goes well it creates a positive image.

If you look cheap, your presentation will be cheap. If you have a high-class presentation, you will come across as high class. It's as simple as that.

BREAK GOALS INTO EASY STEPS

Success is the ability to plan ahead to get the job done. It's breaking it down into steps and making the steps easy projects. I've had jobs that lasted a whole year and it's tough...you sit down and there's so much work here to do that it becomes overwhelming.

There's my office, for instance. When I first bought this building it was a mess, and it's taken me probably two years to finish the place. I've put every nail into it, but not a thing would have been accomplished if I hadn't broken it down into small steps and taken them one at a time.

BUSINESS EXCELLENCE

When I think of business excellence, I keep bumping into ethics. Ethics are what business is all about. Business can be very greedy. I feel there are a lot of people out there with more greed than ethics. To me ethics can be summed up by the golden rule—do unto others as you would have them do unto you. I've been raked over the coals by a lot of people, but I try my best to be as honest as I can.

Business excellence is performance in an arena with business professionals who treat people like people and not as a means to their own end. That is business excellence.

Craig Johnson
The Image Works
2816 T Street
Sacramento, CA 95816
916-456-0747

Steven J. Kitnick

Steven Kitnick is broker-owner of NRS Steve Kitnick Real Estate, a franchise of National Real Estate Service. He has served as honorary mayor of Fair Oaks and is currently on the board of directors of the Fair Oaks Chamber of Commerce. Mr. Kitnick formerly was a top producer for Great Western Real Estate and Lyon & Associates, where he earned numerous awards.

Franchises are popping up like wildflowers after a spring rain. The reason? In sharp contrast to the alarming failure rate of new businesses—seventy percent within the first three years—franchise failure is only ten percent!

The success rate of these types of businesses is high because franchisors start by establishing a pattern of success—proven in real world situations—and then pass the knowledge of how to replicate that winning formula to the franchisee.

It was the marketing system NRS offered that led Steven Kitnick to purchase a franchise. As an international real estate corporation, NRS is a consistent supporter of its franchisees, offering such services as computerized catalog publication, computerized national listing services and personalized marketing material. For example, if an NRS agent is selling a house in Florida and the owners want to buy a property in Sacramento, a check on the national computer system provides quick access to NRS listings.

The same support is available on a local, regional and international level, as well.

All printing and mailing of promotional materials is also handled by NRS, freeing the agent to do what he does best—service his clients. And providing quality service, according to Kitnick, is the essence of a successful operation.

National Real Estate Service is also a company that emphasizes promoting the individual agent. This philosophy meshes perfectly with Kitnick's own marketing style of aggressively promoting the name of Steve Kitnick.

Kitnick bought his NRS franchise in a prime location near the corner of Madison Avenue and Fair Oaks Boule-

"I don't sell real estate, I sell Steve Kitnick. I sell myself, and then provide the best service possible."

"My goal is to

establish an identity in

a targeted market area

so that people will

immediately recognize

my name when they

see it."

vard, where he has experienced rapid growth of his business since he opened his doors in 1988.

Author's Note: When Steve and I got together early in the morning for our interview, we began by making coffee to alert our minds for the task at hand. He had just bought a brand new European style coffee maker and wasn't sure how it worked. I thought I could figure it out, so I gave him directions. As the coffee perked Steve gave me the grand tour of his offices. Ten minutes later we returned to find puddles of coffee on the floor. Realizing that our talents lie outside the realm of foreign contraptions, we shut the damn thing off and went out for coffee!

When it comes to marketing, I don't sell real estate, I sell Steve Kitnick. I sell myself, and then provide the best service possible. I'm hoping people will come to know who I am and what I represent so they'll want to do business with me, and will come back again.

My name and photograph are printed on every piece of marketing literature I send out, and I'm on twenty bus benches along Sunrise Boulevard and Madison Avenue. I look for every opportunity to gain publicity, and I often combine my PR work with community service. For instance, I'm currently on the board of directors for the Fair Oaks Chamber of Commerce.

Marketing through community service may sound a little self-serving, but it depends upon your motive. I join clubs and organizations in which I have a genuine interest and in which I can be of service. It seems to be a natural chain of events to do business with people you know and like.

TARGET MARKETING

When you're starting your business, you have to focus primarily on marketing and promoting yourself. As the business takes off, you keep pressing on the marketing and promotion throttle.

I never cut back on advertising. If anything, I find more ways to step it up. Too often, in a slow market, people in business back up instead of stepping on the accelerator. You have to keep adding fuel to your engine or else it dies and stagnation sets in.

My marketing philosophy is nothing original. It's called *target marketing*. My goal is to establish an identity in a targeted market area so that people will immediately recognize my name when they see it. I do my promoting through various media. My current target market is in the Fair Oaks/Gold River area, and I'm expanding to Citrus Heights and other surrounding areas soon.

"You can't judge success from every at-bat."

SEIZING THE OPPORTUNITY

The biggest obstacle I had to overcome in beginning my business was seizing the opportunity. I felt like I was on the high dive of a swimming pool for the first time. There was no one pushing me off the board—it was up to me alone to take the risk needed to make my dream a reality. And in the end, I literally pulled myself off that plateau and took the plunge into a new adventure!

KEEP YOUR EYE ON THE BALL

If I'm knocking on doors and people don't want to take the time to speak with me, or I'm making cold calls and they hang up on me, I don't take it personally. I draw upon my past experiences to help me maintain belief in myself.

I often think back to an experience I had when I played in an all-star baseball game.

It was the ninth inning with two outs and we were losing.

I felt the pressure of needing to make a hit—to make contact with the ball so that we could have another chance. It wasn't a home run I was shooting for, but a hit.

I walked up to the plate, kicked the dirt off my cleats, took a deep breath and gave it my best. I remember thinking, "Just make contact with the ball. Don't think of anything else. Just make contact!"

I hit a double and gave my team another chance. We

"I don't sell real estate, I provide peace of mind. I am able to do that because I am service-driven. I want people to have enough trust and faith in me to know that I will take care of them."

didn't win, but to me it was a victory. I made contact with the ball, I got a hit and put the team *closer* to victory.

When I meet adversity in my daily business, I often remind myself of that memorable moment. I tell myself not to focus on the goals so much as on making the contact. I know that if I take those little incremental steps that are necessary to achieve the job—making the calls, knocking on doors and making contact—I'm going to generate business.

SUCCESSFUL CONTACTS

That philosophy not only helps me handle rejection on the bad days, but is a key to my success. You can't judge success from every *at-bat*. Just as a baseball player can be inducted into the Hall of Fame by failing to get a base hit seventy percent of the time, I can be a success in business. I can't judge my overall success by the immediate failures.

Absolutely the worst thing that could happen to me when I don't close a deal is that I will learn more about being a good businessman. And that will only make me better next time around. I just concentrate on making the contacts and providing the service and I know I will come through.

PERSPECTIVES ON SUCCESS FROM STEVE KITNICK
- Sharing your vision
- Superior marketing system
- Making contact
- Gambling on yourself
- Results with integrity

A VISION, A DREAM

Before you start to make the contacts, however, you have to have a game plan. To become successful, one must have a dream and a clearly defined goal with a sense of purpose. Once you have defined those things you must have the commitment to carry through.

Then, you need to enlist others to help you realize your dreams. When you are honest and self-disclosing, people are more likely to help you. When others know your motives and objectives, they often enjoy being a part of seeing you attain them.

As you bite off one goal at a time, you will do what's necessary to meet the challenge. As an example, I used to do stand-up comedy, and there were times I would book myself into a room without having an act together. Of course, this forced me to do what was necessary to please the audience.

I still put the horse before the cart sometimes. I often commit myself to buying something for my business and then try to figure out where I'm going to get the money to pay for it. Entrepreneurs are risk takers, but they are risk takers who believe in themselves!

> *"Entrepreneurs are risk takers, but they are risk takers who believe in themselves."*

FINANCIAL INDEPENDENCE FOR THE '90s

By March of 1991, I expect to have twenty agents working with me—not for me. I want them earning and keeping one hundred percent of their commission dollars. As for myself, I plan to phase out of dealing directly with the buyers and sellers and I plan to begin concentrating totally on providing marketing services for my agents.

I want the agents in the field, doing the work and making the money. Many real estate operations penalize their top agents—the more they sell, the more the company takes. Here, there is a flat monthly management fee that doesn't change with the agent's earnings.

DEDICATED PROFESSIONALS

The type of people I want to bring into my business are full-time professionals dedicated to the industry. I want people who are interested in the advancement of their education, who have professional competence and who have high ethical standards. And my agents must also understand the value of self promotion.

I have a slogan that relates my basic business philosophy—*Results with Integrity.* My agents must be committed to that end. Today's top-notch salespeople are trained professionals, matching the client's needs with the product. If the match isn't there, they don't push it.

SELLING PEACE OF MIND

I don't sell real estate, I provide peace of mind. I am able to do that because I am service-driven. I want people to have enough trust and faith in me to know that I will take care of them.

Focusing on the service aspect is analogous to going for the first down in football. Rarely do you get a touchdown at the kick-off. It is a steady succession of first downs that brings you ultimately to the scoring position.

And that is how I judge my success—by the quality of my service, not the money I earn. Through making those service first downs, I have earned a strong referral base and a solid foundation for my business.

A PHILOSOPHICAL OUTLOOK

From the time I was seventeen, I dreamed of earning a college degree in philosophy. I chose philosophy because I wanted a good education, a solid learning experience. I truly believe that in the long run, the most successful people possess a strong liberal arts background.

I left college at nineteen and returned to complete my degree at age twenty-four. I remember that first semester back. I had an anxiety attack in my philosophy class. I couldn't believe that I had three more years to get through, and questioned what I was even doing in the class.

So, once again, I had my vision—to graduate. And I set my goals in first down increments. I took my college attendance one day at a time, and sometimes one lecture at a time. By focusing on the present, I was able to achieve success. I won several awards, including Most Outstanding Male Graduate. I never sought these distinctions out, they came to me because of my ability to do my best daily.

People used to ask, me what I could possibly do with a degree in philosophy, and I replied, "Laminate it!" The effects of my education may not be immediately apparent in my profession, but my philosophy course work greatly increased my skills to read, write, think, listen and feel. From there, my abilities have allowed me to expand my business communication and problem-solving capabilities.

GAMBLE ON YOURSELF

Betting on a football game is a risky proposition. Too many games are decided by turnovers. You never know how that funny-shaped ball is going to bounce when it's fumbled.

However, when I fumble the ball, it always bounces right back to me. That's why I bet on myself!

National Real Estate Service
NRS Steve Kitnick Real Estate
8080 Madison Ave., Suite 102-A
Fair Oaks, CA 95628
Business: 916-965-5500
Fax: 916-537-0460

C. Arthur McBride was an executive with the Dun & Bradstreet Corporation for fourteen years prior to starting his numismatic firm early in 1989. He earned a bachelor's degree from the University of Vermont in 1973. He is a member of the American Numismatic Association and the Society for United States Commemorative Coins, as well as Florida United Numismatists.

Many of us view the average coin collector as a person who fills up volume after volume of cardboard books with old pennies, dimes and nickels found in pockets or drawers. Although collectors of this type still exist, they are becoming the minority as Wall Street's well-heeled professionals enter the game.

Today the hobby of coin collecting has become big business for many people. Million dollar bids for coins are made at auctions, and daily trading is often done through a computer network. Coin shows are also extremely popular, as astronomical sums of money change hands at these weekend events. While some people are collecting rare coins as pieces of historical art, others are continually trading coins as they would stocks on the New York Stock Exchange.

The events surrounding the resurgence of the industry center on the revolutionary changes that occurred only a few years ago. Now, the product sold by most dealers is guaranteed not only by them, but by a third party service, significantly reducing risk to the consumer.

Handling numismatic investments in this increasingly sophisticated industry requires a lot more today than a good eye and a knowledge of current bullion values. It requires an ability to merge coins, clients and technology into an investment portfolio.

Therefore, the new breed of numismatic professional must have a sophisticated understanding of financial plans and goals, as well as the professionalism to deal with today's successful investors.

That is where Art McBride saw his opportunity. After eighteen years of successfully investing in coins as a hobby, McBride left an executive position with Dun & Bradstreet, a Fortune 500 business services organization,

"When I was a resident (of Vermont), there were literally more cows than people."

"...working for Dun & Bradstreet for six months is the equivalent of two years in graduate school."

to turn his hobby into a career.

One year after moving to Sacramento and starting an appraisal, counseling and coin service, McBride's business is prospering. With clients from coast to coast, he spends much of his time on the road, in search of the rarest and most beautiful coins to place in the portfolios of his eclectic clientele.

Author's Note: *When Art McBride and I met for his interview, he showed me a small oblong box containing about thirty shiny pieces of history. Although these rare coins from the turn of the century were valued at more than $8,000, Art spoke of his appreciation of the beauty of the coins' appearance in a way that transcended cash value.*

I grew up on an island in Vermont, surrounded by Lake Champlain. The state of Vermont is not very densely populated. In fact, the latest rumor is that there are now more people than cows. When I was a resident, however, there were literally more cows than people. After I graduated from the University of Vermont in 1973, it was evident that I would have to move to a metropolitan area if I wanted a career with growth potential.

I chose Dallas, Texas to begin my professional career. At that time, the oil boom was just starting, and a thousand people a week were moving to the Dallas area. I went to work for a finance company to get some business experience and then moved on to Dun & Bradstreet, where I remained for fourteen years. My last position was Southwest district manager, based in Phoenix. I was responsible for the states of Arizona and New Mexico and had approximately fifty people reporting to me. The information resources division, which I was part of, was responsible for writing comprehensive credit reports on businesses throughout the world.

THE CORPORATE CHALLENGE

That was an education, because working for Dun & Bradstreet for six months is the equivalent of two years in graduate school. The analysts speak only with owners, presidents and partners of companies—the people who determine how a company operates, how well it's doing, why business is up or down and all the nitty-gritty. Basically, Dun & Bradstreet operates as a credit executive for vendors.

All of the jobs at D&B are extremely challenging. When I talk about challenge, I am also talking about a high level of pressure. Everyone within the corporation has a weekly quota to meet. Analysts are expected to interview a certain number of business principals, compile the information, write reports and submit them weekly. Once in management, as most managers in the company point out, you have one hundred and five objectives that you must meet every Friday afternoon. If you make one hundred and three, nobody cares; they want to know why you didn't make the other two.

For me the challenges had a very positive impact. Succeeding at D&B gave me the confidence of knowing that if I could achieve at that job, I could achieve on my own. I have always been a self-starter anyway, and learning about other businesses that failed or prospered gave me the courage to finally go out on my own.

"Once in management, as most managers in the company point out, you have one hundred and five objectives that you must meet every Friday afternoon. If you make one hundred and three, nobody cares; they want to know why you didn't make the other two."

EARLY INTEREST
When I was a kid, I was a coin collector. I guess most of us were. Around 1980, when gold was $800 an ounce and silver was $50 an ounce, I pulled out my coin collection and got back into buying, selling and trading coins.

I started buying more investment quality coins from some very reputable dealers in the Dallas area, who sat me down and explained how to grade a coin.

MAKING THE GRADE
Grading—which determines the quality of a coin—was very much an individual thing during the precious metals boom. There was no consistent approach to coin grading or the value that should be applied to a particular coin. Several different dealers would often have as many opinions.

Also during that time, there were many unscrupulous dealers selling coins to the unsuspecting public, claiming that a coin was uncirculated and in a certain condition. Customers would later find out that coins had been cleaned and polished—two things which actually devalue

"...learning so much about businesses that failed or prospered gave me the courage to finally go out on my own."

them. Consequently, the rare coin industry developed a somewhat tarnished reputation.

THE REVOLUTION

In 1986, the industry was revolutionized and I started to contemplate entering the coin business. Several of the leading dealers in the United States got together and decided to develop some guidelines to ensure survival of the industry by offering consumer protection.

They formed a corporation called Professional Coin Grading Services (PCGS), which grades and authenticates rare coins. Every coin is examined by a minimum of four experts, who themselves are required to pass stringent tests. Once a coin is graded, it is sealed in a plastic holder and PCGS guarantees that the coin is correctly graded and authentic.

In this way, the value of many coins today is no longer just in the hands of the dealer.

PERSPECTIVES ON SUCCESS FROM ART McBRIDE
- Dun & Bradstreet
- Buying, selling and trading
- Coin grading
- American Numismatic Exchange
- Rare coins as history
- Mints yield jackpots

THE NUMBERS GAME

Grading of coins has also led to cataloguing, so we now have a much better idea of which coins are really rare. Before statistics were kept, dealers might have said, "This coin is extremely rare. It's undervalued. You should buy it."

In many cases they were correct, but then in a lot of cases they were wrong. Today, anyone can buy a population report that lists rare coins. Even the novice collector can sit down with a pricing guide and figure out what's undervalued.

EXCHANGING BIDS

The population report and the grading system have given people a more consistent approach to rare coin investing, while another innovation has made trading much easier. The American Numismatic Exchange (ANE) is a computerized network for trading coins graded by PCGS. Where dealers once had to call every dealer they knew or scour coin shows, they can now search for many coins through the system.

In addition, ANE dealers post daily bidding and asking prices on coins in which they specialize, while top bidders are required to purchase coins at the bid price, sight unseen. At a glance, dealers know who is paying the highest prices in the United States. The increased liquidity that the system promotes for dealers and investors alike has caused many to enter the market for the first time—including Kidder-Peabody, Shearson-Lehman and Merrill Lynch.

With these three innovations in place, I could not resist the market any longer. I proceeded to learn all I could about the coin industry from a dealer's perspective, and in 1989 I dove in!

"There was no consistent approach to coin grading or the value that should be applied to a particular coin."

LEARNING THE GAME

No one can succeed or survive in the coin industry without friends. Therefore it's very important to develop a rapport with other dealers to keep abreast of news, as well as locate special coins for clients.

I have met some great people in the industry, but one person has been especially instrumental in my success.

About the time I began to consider coins as a profession, I met Mark Machin of American Federal Rare Coin & Bullion. Mark willingly spent hours, over a two-year period, teaching me the intricacies of the new coin market. Because of him, I was prepared when I finally made the transition to numismatics as a profession.

BUILDING THE FOUNDATION

As a general rule, seasoned numismatic professionals have a set client base they have been dealing with for years and many of them don't market themselves at all. Some of them just have a very good reputation for treating people fairly and they work on referral alone.

Even as a relative newcomer to the industry, I have chosen to build my client base primarily through referrals. It may be slower in the beginning, but for me, it's a way to ensure a solid customer foundation from which to branch out. I have some marketing plans for 1990, but I will target small groups of people in certain professional environments rather than the general public.

THE BIRTH OF A COLLECTOR

Our clients come in three types. Many are long time collectors—people who buy a coin every few months. Some are investors—people who hold on to coins for a year or two and sell them when they appreciate to a certain point. Then we also have market players—people who buy and sell weekly, somewhat like options trading.

I enjoy dealing with the collectors as much as, if not more than, the investors. It's really satisfying to find the last puzzle piece for someone who is trying to put a collection together.

Another enjoyable aspect of the job is turning the investor into a collector. Once an investor takes physical possession of a coin, he often looks at the coin in a new light—not just as a money-making device. He begins to appreciate that this coin is a hundred years old, has never been circulated, and it probably came from someone else's collection, started long ago.

HANG ON FOR THE RIDE

Aside from their aesthetic value, rare coins are a great investment. And it doesn't necessarily require thousands of dollars to start a collection. Certified coins can be purchased for as little as $15. Although many of my clients buy one coin a month, others make a lump sum purchase of several thousand dollars a year, similar to an IRA.

Anyone considering becoming a market player, though, definitely needs a strong heart because it's very volatile on a daily and weekly basis. We've been through some violent price fluctuations just in the last year (1989). From January through the first week of June, the price on a lot of coins went up one hundred percent or more. Later in June and July many of them came down in price to what they are today. Anyone who bought into the market in January and sold out in May did very, very well.

CRUNCHING THE NUMBERS

I use a lot of statistical analysis to determine the best buys and the best time to buy and sell for my clients. I study the population versus current price and past price per-formance. I've really found some undervalued bargains by performing computer-generated analyses of various coins.

Investing has evolved into a somewhat simpler process because the collector has the same information as the dealer. There are really no secrets since anybody can sit down with the pricing guides.

Generally speaking, though, the higher the quality, the better the price performance has always been. You can't fight the trends in the industry. For instance, there are coins in high grades that sold in 1980 for $200 that are now selling for $5,000. The coins that sold for $10 in 1980 are now selling at $20. As a rule, the greater the rarity factor, the better the chance for price appreciation.

"...the industry was revolutionized and I started to contemplate entering the coin business."

PEOPLE WHO COUNT

The biggest obstacle I faced in starting my business was being sure in my own mind that I would succeed once I was in, although I never looked back. My wife, Barrett, has supported my plans even when we decided to pack up and move to Sacramento. She had to give up her job and move to an area she had never seen. It was her confidence in me that really relieved me of any lingering self-doubt.

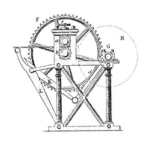

Once established, my first hurdle in building a business was acquiring a client base and becoming part of a dealer network. It is crucial to develop a following in this industry and to know the right people. There are several dealers in the coin industry whom I respect very much. Their ethical responsibility is high so you know that if they tell you something, it's true. In this self-regulated industry, inside information goes a long way.

Inventory sources are also necessary. For instance, if I need a coin, I have to know who deals in it. The dealer may be in New York, in Florida, or he might be here in California. Without that information, business would be extremely difficult to conduct.

IS YOUR HOBBY WORKING?

On an immediate level, success to me is making money for my clients. On a more personal level, I am successful because I have the ability to make my living in a profession which was my hobby. I don't see how anyone could ask for more! It is very enjoyable.

I sell a product which I can see, study and enjoy. Also, my product is an attractive piece of history. How many people in the sales profession can say that?

TAKING THE TIME TO TEACH

The main reason I have achieved success in a short period of time is that I take the time to educate people. I

"The increased liquidity that the system promotes for dealers and investors alike has caused many to enter the market for the first time— including Kidder-Peabody, Shearson-Lehman and Merrill Lynch."

talk to a lot of people who tell me they have run into many dealers who really just want to sell them a coin and will not take the time to give them any extra information.

I tell people the rationale behind my suggestion to buy a certain coin, having found that if you take your time with people, they will come back to you.

The reason I feel confident with my investment suggestions is based on my experience. I may not have been in the business for twenty years, but I have been actively buying, selling and learning for almost that long and I am very knowledgeable. I know my subject well.

A BOOMING BUSINESS

For 1990, I expect my sales volume to increase three or fourfold. The training year for me was 1989. I learned a lot, developed an established base and it is paying off. The only real strategy I am changing is to concentrate more on the higher end of the market, trying to deal in even rarer coins. They are a higher price, but they consistently outperform other coins and are in great demand for collections.

For the next two to five years, I am planning to continue growth at controlled levels—again so I maintain a solid customer base. I never envision my business expanding to the point that I have salesmen working for me. It is quite lucrative and enjoyable as a one man show!

A HEALTHY CLIMATE

The best way to describe the business climate in Sacramento is to say that it is very receptive. That is why I chose to start my business here. There are many avid collectors here because of the close proximity to two mints—San Francisco and Carson City, where millions of silver dollars are available to collectors as well as casinos.

The people here, in general, are receptive to new businesses also, because the city is prospering by its growth.

AN HISTORICAL OUTLOOK

Perhaps I find history fascinating because my family has
been in Vermont for over two hundred years. Having
such an old American heritage meant that I grew up
learning about my ancestors. It also meant that in addition to my very supportive parents, I had the security of
relatives scattered throughout the island. That solid
background has been instrumental in my ability to
prosper in the wake of life's many transitions. I am glad I
landed in Sacramento, and I am looking forward to
growing with this beautiful part of California!

Art McBride
P.O. Box 1061
Fair Oaks, CA 95628
916-961-1452

Robert C. McCann

Lisa Alcock

Robert McCann *is the founder of The Logical Choice Inc., a management consulting firm based in the Cameron Park area. For over ten years, he has been working with business owners and managers bringing them to new levels of performance, results and productivity through communication and team building. Bob has an extensive background in business negotiation, consultative selling and conflict resolution.* **Lisa Alcock** *was a commercial real estate property manager prior to joining the firm as vice president and marketing director.*

I n sports, the ability a coach has to manage his or her players often determines the outcome of the game. But did you ever consider that in the game of business, the skills you possess to motivate others directly impact your win-loss ratio? Bob McCann and Lisa Alcock have successfully applied the basic principles of coaching to the special needs of a diversity of businesses.

Their unique approach to management consulting has facilitated positive changes in a local prison system, as well as in manufacturing firms, high tech companies and sales organizations. They have been called in to ease the work-place transition that occurs in the aftermath of an acquisition, as well as to facilitate communication between two firms contemplating a merger. Their approach is universally applicable because of their objective—to help clients realize their needs and *act* to achieve their goals. The concept is simple, the process often agonizing, and the outcome always enlightening.

According to McCann, much research has gone into discovering the secrets that winning athletic coaches use to gain success for their players. This research has been transferred into conceptual models that can be used to replicate the same success in business. "Distinctions" are important concepts to the coaching approach. Without them, say McCann and Alcock, teamwork and maximum utilization of human resources will not occur within a company. For instance, great coaches avoid telling players how to do everything. Instead, they coach them to see new "openings." New opportunities enable them to choose an appropriate action, given their intention, their unique abilities and the task before them. When San Francisco 49ers quarterback Joe Montana is in the pocket looking down field, he's not recalling the coach's instructions, he's seeking openings for action.

"Our business is by no means a typical management consulting service...We actually set up transition projects which alter the internal culture, as well as the performance of a company, while producing specific measurable business results."

"Our retreats operate as strategic planning sessions with a heavy emphasis on strengthening relationships and clarifying specific goals within the business."

McCann and Alcock have seen great success among the firms that retain them to aid in the achievement of specific long-term objectives. In addition, The Logical Choice offers a variety of workshops including Critical Success Strategies and The Art of Consultative Selling. A third and very powerful workshop—Balance in Business—is the result of Alcock's commitment to the balance between hard work and quality of life, according to McCann. And a fourth workshop, called Couples in Business, was spawned by this couple's solid working and personal relationship.

The Logical Choice also offers client-specific retreats and strategic planning meetings. Whether McCann and Alcock are facilitating a retreat or meeting with a client one-on-one, their primary goal is to act as a coach. And that means to help clients define their special needs and to see them through the actions necessary to achieve a specific goal—be it selling the company, increasing the sales or improving employee relations.

Author's Note: *The "coaching" approach to business management offered by McCann and Alcock isn't taught at Stanford University. It is on the leading edge of successful management technology and is becoming an integral part of the winning business strategy for a growing number of firms. McCann's proven track record demonstrates the benefits of this technology.*

BOB: Our business is by no means a typical management consulting service since we focus primarily on providing what we like to call "cultural coaching." We actually set up transition projects which alter the internal culture, as well as the performance of a company, while producing specific measurable business results. On a basic level, we help companies create an environment so that communication among all parties remains effective.

Our clients usually start out in one of our public workshops or they hire us to facilitate a retreat. From there, we are often retained to handle long-term projects of a given company. Our retreats operate as strategic planning sessions with a heavy emphasis on strengthening relationships and clarifying specific goals within the business. We focus on correcting the bad communication habits that have emerged within a firm.

AN ACQUISITION WITH A HAPPY ENDING

BOB: I'll give you an example of how our approach brought desirable results to a client. We were retained by a distributing company to facilitate the sale of the business. One of our assignments was to determine the market value of the business, including the intangibles.

Before we had finished our assessment, an offer was made to purchase the business. Once we completed our study, it took only one meeting with the buyer to elicit a proposal that was double the original offer. Because we worked openly, with all of our client's needs and concerns on the table, the buyer and the seller of the company were able to develop a trust for each other, which resulted in a partnership between the two! We were later retained by the buyer to facilitate the merger of two national sales divisions.

INTROSPECTION

BOB: In sports, coaching often involves watching a player perform—looking for the flaws in his performance as an outside observer. In the stands it's much easier to see what he needs to do differently to be successful, but the athlete is often blind to the flaw in his game.

We do the same thing for business people that coaches do for athletes. We actually get people to view themselves in action so they see what's not working for them. Then they use us as a sounding board to formulate a winning plan of action. We don't look for mistakes—we help our clients see for themselves.

When CEOs, for example, take that seat in the stands, they begin to recognize how the rules of the game have changed since they first started out in business. The key to an entrepreneur's success in the early stages is controlling the environment. He takes pride in doing the majority of the work himself, and he works with a very small group of people.

Once the firm achieves some success, all that begins to change. All the habits he needed to become successful

"We actually get people to view themselves in action so they see what's not working for them. Then, they use us as a sounding board to formulate a winning plan of action."

"When CEOs, for example, take that seat in the stands, they begin to recognize how the rules of the game have changed since they first started out in business."

in the first place are exactly the habits that inhibit the business to reach higher levels. He has to learn to let go of the control which was the key to his early achievement. That is a very difficult thing for most people to do, but it is essential to achieve the successful transition from a start-up to a stable business.

LISA: For instance, a manager in a growth company may come to us, exasperated with his employees, because he has trouble with delegation. He'll say, "I don't know why they don't grasp what they are supposed to do. Nobody seems to be able to do anything as well as I can. They're just not getting it." It's as though he knows what he wants, but he can't understand why his employees don't. It becomes an us-against-them relationship, with a lot of built-in alienation and frustration on both sides.

BOB: Both managers and employees need to alter the fundamental way they think about their business and their business relationships. Coaching helps them accomplish that by teaching them to acquire a new perspective on their actions.

PERSPECTIVES ON SUCCESS
FROM BOB McCANN AND LISA ALCOCK

- CEOs and coaches
- Healthy communication
- Tell the truth
- What's missing from this picture?
- What are *you* up to in business?
- Ultimate personal integrity

TEAMING UP AGAINST ALIENATION

LISA: It's very successful. When I came to work with Bob, we went back and interviewed past clients, finding the one continuous thread that was woven into each owner's conversation. Before our project, each owner had the same type of conversation. They'd say, "I don't know what it's going to take. My employees just don't do what I want, and I'm frustrated. What do I do, fire them?" At the same time the employees would tell us, "I don't know what the owner wants." Both sides were entirely alienated from one another.

After the project, each business became a team. The owners were able to share their vision of what kind of company they wanted, and then transfer that to their people with a lot of conditions for satisfaction that were then met. Employees could now say, "Oh! This is what she wants!" They could see how they could contribute to making that vision a reality. They had jumped the alienation fence.

MOVING UP THE LADDER OF ACKNOWLEDGMENT

BOB: There's a school of management that says when you acknowledge people for doing a good job, you're ruining their motivation to take on what's next. The truth is that the only time people will take on what's next with vigor and real enthusiasm is after their work has been fully acknowledged. By acknowledgment, we mean telling the truth in a way that supports the employee's position in the company—that includes communicating the negatives. People really appreciate the truth in the long run. It's a clear way to operate and it allows much more room for growth, progress and healthy change.

Stroking employees sparingly is very counter-productive to their effectiveness. Envision a ladder as you step from one rung up to the next. You can't do that by jumping forward with two feet. You've got to take it slowly—one step at a time. Without acknowledgment of the truth and the deserved pats on the back, the lower foot will remain on the bottom rung. It's easy to see that this acknowledgment is a very basic key to improving communication between employers and employees.

At the same time, not acknowledging a negative performance by an employee is just as damaging to employer/employee communication.

LEARNING TO ASK QUESTIONS WITHOUT ANSWERS

BOB: Typically, people with problems ask what's wrong, what's not working, or what do I have to do to contribute? Seldom do they stand back from the immediate, look at their concerns in their business and ask, "What's missing from this picture?"

Solutions are found only by asking the right questions. As strange as it sounds, you have to be willing to create questions that are not intended to get a specific answer. You have to ask questions which open up a fresh perspective. This makes people uncomfortable because, first, it seems very strange to ask a question that is not designed for a specific answer; and second, such questions inevitably reveal your own ignorance.

"Both managers and employees need to alter the fundamental way they think about their business and their business relationships."

"The owners were able to share their vision of what kind of company they wanted, and then transfer that to their people with a lot of conditions for satisfaction that were then met."

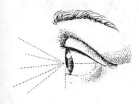

It's uncomfortable for people to confront their own lack of knowledge, especially when it concerns their own lives—the direction they're heading and the things they are doing to get there. We, in essence, invite people to momentarily turn their backs to the amount of new information that is continually pouring in as we begin to ask questions that open up awareness.

A VISION OF TRUTH
BOB: The one big secret to success is to be clearly focused on what you want to do. Be clear that the reason you want to do it is because it is the expression of who you are, not just a way to get rich. That's the hard part.

The next trick is to stay true to that vision no matter what. If you are very clear that your business is an expression of who you are and it provides value to your customers, nothing can hold you down. We spend about four hours on this topic in one of our workshops. When it becomes clear in your own mind that where you're going in business is an expression of who you are, you can stay focused on that vision even when the crowd says it won't work.

Finally, to be successful, it is also extremely important to have truthful relationships with people. Don't just go along with their fantasies. Tell them the truth.

THE ULTIMATE INTEGRITY QUOTIENT
BOB: Your level of truthfulness in business is what we call your integrity quotient. If I'm interested in a relationship, whether it be business or personal, I have to bring to that relationship my own personal integrity. Improving business relationships means improving our own integrity. If both partners in the relationship have a high level of integrity, the relationship itself will be fulfilling for both parties.

I know that the most important thing I can bring to the party, in any relationship, is honesty. We're speaking of business relationships and excellence, too. I have to focus on my personal integrity by keeping my promises with that other person or business. That's how I try to approach everything. I believe that is the best way to do business and the best way to live.

THE CHANCE OF A LIFETIME

BOB: One man's integrity changed my life. In 1979, I was a computer management consultant with a firm in San Francisco. Roy Toms, owner of a large independent distributorship of Exxon products in the U.S. and one of my firm's clients, approached me with a deal that I thank him for to this day.

He wanted me to become independent and provide my consulting services to his company. The deal was that he would hire me for six months as an independent consultant, while I worked on a business plan to start my own consulting firm.

Roy has done the same thing for many other entre-preneurs. He has this mission to bring together people who are committed to serving in business. He wants to help put them in a position where they can start their own companies and operate on their own. Roy gets a lot of personal satisfaction out of making a contribution to people who are committed to serving others. He operates on a level of integrity that is extraordinary.

His offer was the turning point for me. In 1980 I made the transition from working strictly with computers to consulting with businesses on their relationships with other computer vendors. I helped my clients manage their own projects rather than just telling them what to do from a technical standpoint, which led me into consulting outside the domain of computers. I finally had the opportunity to do what I'm best at—helping businesses and business owners accomplish their goals and become more successful.

In 1984, after four years of management consulting, I adopted the coaching technique. Although the traditional approach of researching, observing and suggesting tactics satisfied my clients, I found that far greater results were achieved and—more importantly—maintained when I helped my clients discover solutions for themselves.

"...the only time people will take on what's next with vigor and real enthusiasm is after their work has been fully acknowledged. By acknowledgment we mean telling the truth in a way that supports the employee's position in the company."

APPLYING THE SKILLS

LISA: When people concentrate on their own personal integrity, we find there is a direct impact not only on their business lives, but on how they run their personal lives as well. For instance, one of our clients took me aside just last week to tell me what a difference coaching had made in a personal relationship with her husband. "I've been using the skills you've taught me, and the result has been the best conversation I have ever had with my husband!" she said.

She was able to use the skills we taught her to improve her whole life. This is what is so rewarding about the work we do. The working relationships that we build with our clients are very special and long lasting. We have the privilege of contributing to many aspects of our clients' lives.

BOB: When people engage in one of our workshops, they walk out with a new perspective of the world. They take that new perspective into their family and business lives.

Success is being able to thrive in my business and to contribute to the betterment of individuals. Through them will come the betterment of the world.

Bob McCann
Lisa Alcock
The Logical Choice Inc.
2621 Crowdis Lane
Rescue, CA 95672
916-989-0463

Robbie Motter
*is a marketing
consultant and owner
of Contacts Unlimited,
the company that puts
people in business
together and special-
izes in both the federal
and commercial
markets. Ms. Motter
has more than twenty-
five years of experi-
ence in administration,
accounting and
procurement manage-
ment and is in constant
demand as a talk show
guest, keynote speaker
and seminar leader.*

Robbie Motter is a dynamo. Her accomplishments are so numerous that her resumé approaches the magnitude of a James Michener novel. She is featured in virtually every *Who's Who* book in the country and heads up committees on dozens of local, as well as national, service and professional organizations.

"...I'm on a side road again."

She is a member of the Republican President's Commission and was nominated by Senator Robert Dole to be a member of the Republican Senatorial Inner Circle. She is also on the President's Task Force.

She does that, in addition to overseeing a national marketing company that assists small and large businesses in obtaining their fair share of the $60 billion government marketplace.

Robbie's boundless energy benefits all who know and work with her. Her philosophy is to help men and women succeed in life by realizing all their personal dreams and business goals. She works with new and small businesses to develop marketing strategies and publicity for business growth.

In this chapter you'll learn what makes Robbie—and her clients—so successful.

Author's Note: *Always the polite business executive, Robbie asked her secretary to hold all phone calls during our interview. After we had covered all the pertinent points about her business and the success she has achieved, I still felt something was missing. I still hadn't discovered the essence of her personality, the driving force that made her*

"...the gut feeling...like

an inner person who

knows you better than

anyone else."

successful. Just before I left, she pointed to a wall full of awards for her achievements. She said, "Although I appreciate all this, these are not my most cherished awards." She then brought out letters and poems written by former business associates. She read each and every one of them to me and, before she finished, tears had welled in the corners of her eyes. Then I understood. Excerpts from a few of these tributes are at the end of this chapter.

One of the greatest qualities I possess is that I can meet people, feel their needs, and move with them. I know exactly how to make a presentation to them. I have a strong intuition which I rely on in everything I do. I think if people look into their lives they'll find that they've had that same feeling and then talked themselves out of doing something only to regret it later. I always say, "Go with the gut feeling; it's like an inner person who knows you better then anyone else." It says what's right for you. You've got to go with it.

CONTACTS AND COUNSELING

Contacts Unlimited is a company that works with manufacturers primarily, but also with service companies. The primary focus is to help them break into the state, federal, and local government markets. From this have come a lot of companies that say, "Gee, you've been so successful doing that. Can you help me in my business? I'm not interested in government, but I just want to know the path to take with my business." I've ended up sitting down and counseling people in small businesses.

YOU CAN'T TAKE A WRONG TURN

I grew up in Hawaii and got my start in business working for one of the most brilliant men in the world. In 1956 at the age of twenty-one I was his Hawaiian Village Hotel's first director of personnel. This man was the first major influence on my life.

At the time, he was building the Kaiser Aluminum Dome for the premiere of *Around the World in Eighty Days*. It was a big aluminum dome with theater seats. One morning I happened to be riding the elevator with him and a couple of his crew members. They were telling Mr. Kaiser that part of his plans wouldn't work, and what he said to them has stayed with me all my life.

He said, "I don't pay you to say it can't be done. You get paid to have it done. I want it done. It can be done. So don't come back to me until it is done!" And boy, that was powerful because I'd never heard anybody make statements like those. As he got out of the elevator he said, "Robbie let this be a lesson to you. Nothing in this world is impossible if you want it. If you want it and others say it cannot be done, don't believe them." That has stayed with me all of my life. Another statement he made also has remained with me—"What the mind can perceive you can achieve!"

Henry J. Kaiser was seventy-six years old at the time. He was the Kaiser of Kaiser ships and Kaiser Permanente. He was the man who produced a car called the Kaiser.

Later in my life, I worked for another influential gentleman in Omaha who taught me a neat thing. He said that life's road is a main highway, but every once in a while we get off on side roads and we get frustrated. We should remember all side roads go back to a main highway. All you have to say to yourself is "oh, I'm on a side road again. I need to get back on the main highway." I've used that philosophy every time I find that things aren't going right and it works!

"Actually it was the Supreme Court that ruled in our favor for other organizations which were challenged."

OPTIMISTIC ENCOUNTERS

One thing that keeps me positive is my involvement in the Optimist Club, a very positive organization. It was founded in 1911 and there are one hundred, eighty-two thousand members all over the country. About three years ago they finally let women in. Actually it was the Supreme Court that ruled in our favor for other organizations which were challenged.

I think I was probably one of the first woman members in Sacramento. I was in the organization for a year and then the next year I was president. I was one of three woman presidents that year in our district of eighty-two clubs. I'm also the first female lieutenant governor in the district.

"It's my belief that everyone should belong to one service club, whatever their choice may be."

I really feel the good that they do—how they work with kids, their bicycle safety, and "Just say no" programs. That's why I became a member.

It's my belief that everyone should belong to one service club, whatever their choice may be. If you don't like working with kids there's a service club that works with the elderly or you can find one that does projects. I like working with kids because I feel that they're going to be up there some day and if they can look back and say, "When I was growing up, adults were mentors to me," then those kids are going to be mentors for the younger ones coming up under them.

For the last three years I have been fortunate to be a part of the Sacramento County Mentor Program. You are matched with a student in one of the high schools and you invite the student to spend the day with you and to come to your place of business. In addition to that, I am a member of the Foundation for Blind Babies Families.

PERSPECTIVES ON SUCCESS FROM ROBBIE MOTTER
- An inner voice
- Mentor program
- Nothing slides
- A gold Mercedes
- Staying in touch
- Joint Chiefs of Staff

GAMBLING WITH THE CASH FLOW
In the five years I have had my own business, money has been the biggest obstacle. Sometimes, whatever you take in, you put back out. I work a lot with small businesses that don't have a lot of money. Often I will front more than I should, but I think of it as a gamble. If they win, I'm going to win. So I don't look at it from a money standpoint so much. I just want to help.

THE MONDAY RULE
The key to getting a lot accomplished in your life is good time management. A rule that I live by is that every Monday morning I make a list of everything I will accomplish that week. I never let anything slide. If I get involved in projects and the list is still incomplete by Saturday, then I work all night to get it done. I find that if you don't get it done, you find reasons to let it go into the next week.

You need to prioritize your list. If you're in business, you do the things that are going to keep your business going first, and fit the other things in. Move everything forward a little bit every day. I'm writing two books, for example, so I take one hour every day to work on each of them.

"...you walk in the door and within two minutes your song is being played."

MARIO THE REMARKABLE

When I relax, I enjoy semiclassical music and light opera. I especially love going to Aldo's Restaurant to listen to Mario, a remarkable pianist in his seventies. He used to head up the Genoa, Italy opera, and when you go in it's like being at a concert.

What's incredible about Mario is that you may not go there for five months, but you walk in the door and within two minutes your song is being played. The man is brilliant. I look at him and he reminds me very much of Mr. Kaiser because he's in his seventies and very alert. I want to be like that—to believe that age doesn't matter. It's what you do with your mind and how you let it grow that makes a difference.

VISUALIZING THE MERCEDES

Never a day goes by that I don't listen to motivational tapes. When I find myself at a point where I think, "Oh my God, am I gonna get through this?" I flop the tape in.

I happen to like Dennis Waitley and Tom Hopkins. They encourage motivation and self-esteem. Now I'm listening to and reading *Think and Grow Rich*. I have it on tape and it's very powerful.

One of the things that comes out in almost all motivational books is perseverance—never giving up. That to me is one of the key tools to success. If it doesn't work today it might work tomorrow, but don't give up. Look at Einstein. He lived many years and he was not a success until he was an old man.

If you want something to work it will work, but you have to visualize yourself seeing it work. For example, for five years before I bought my Mercedes I saw myself driving that car. I had a Lincoln which broke down one day. I thought at the time, "I really can't afford this car, but I'm going to go in and see if I can get it. If I can, it means that I should have it." And I got it!

I broke down the cost to hours and I realized I just needed to make one more sale a week which was easy to

"...for five years

before I bought my

Mercedes I saw myself

driving that car."

do. Sometimes if we look at the big picture it scares us, but if you bring it down to its simplest mode you find that you can solve your problem.

YOURS FOR THE ASKING

It seems that we were raised not to ask for anything because we're bothering people, but that's wrong. In fact, one of the books I am writing addresses this issue.

The bottom line is that we go to places and we meet people, but we never clearly define what we're looking for that will help us. I think we need to do that because every person we meet has a network of people.

You must believe that you can ask people for something and you don't necessarily have to pay them back because you know you're going to help someone else. You soon realize that as long as you give people what they ask for and you help other people, you don't need to feel guilty or owe somebody.

The goal is to help one another grow successfully. So many people are worried about their competitors, but your competitors can help you a lot. Don't be afraid of your competitors; help one another. You can grow together. There's enough business for everybody out there. I work a lot with my competitors. I'm not afraid of them because I know I can't cover the whole market. Yet I can learn from their mistakes, and they can learn from mine.

MIRRORING AN IMAGE

In order to go anywhere in life, you have to believe in yourself, because if you don't believe in yourself, you can't project yourself. I was very shy ten years ago. I always felt that maybe I was inferior to other people. A man I worked for made me stand in front of mirrors everyday and say, "Hey, world. Here I am and I'm wonderful!" I started believing that, and then I began to believe that I could do a lot of good for people. That's what I do in my business today. I help people and that's why I like it. It's very gratifying.

GETTING THE WORD OUT

The fundamental concept to marketing is getting your name out there because people buy from people they know and like. People also like success stories. You may not be that successful, but if people perceive you as successful, they'll do business with you. They don't like dealing with losers; therefore, you have to make yourself a winner.

Direct mail is one way to do that. The law of averages says when you use the direct mail approach, the first time you mail out, the letter may end up in the trash. The second time it may end up in the trash. The third time the name becomes recognizable and they don't remember that they threw it in the trash twice. They're thinking, "Where did I meet this person?" So it stays on their desk. The fourth time the name is instilled in their memory.

I also advise companies to write press releases. I encourage them to introduce themselves to the media.

If you're into health products, find out who the health editors of the local newspapers are, and introduce yourself to them. Send them press releases.

If you're speaking to a group, send a press release that you're speaking. If you've had a huge sale, then do a press release. Try to tie in some things you do with charity, because through charity you can use a lot of public service announcements.

I was talking recently to a man I used to know from Toastmasters who is now vice president of the National Speaker's Association. I had a man in my office who wanted to join, so I made the phone call for him. He said,"You know Robbie, it doesn't matter where I go in this town, I hear your name." People will come up to me that I haven't met and say, "Every place I go people say I should meet you!"

Four years ago I arrived in this town from Washington, D. C., knowing only my mother and father. As my parents lived in Roseville, I moved my business here. My mother was not feeling well and I was an only child. I made a decision in a week to pack up and that meant moving a business and everything. I left all my furniture for my daughter in Virginia and I just came here with my clothes, my younger daughter and a few knick-knacks. We had nothing, but it was important to be here and school was getting ready to start. There wasn't time to think about it.

SPEAKING NATURALLY

I joined Toastmasters here to improve my speaking abilities and I was petrified of speaking. I did several small talks and I received great critiques. One of the

"The goal is to help one another grow successfully."

"Don't be afraid of your competitors; help one another."

things I found was that I'm what you call a natural speaker, so I decided that Toastmasters was not for me.

People who have seen my writing feel that I'm very creative and to take a structured course would ruin my writing. Well, I speak the same way. I have ideas, but when I get to the group it's how I talk that gets people excited. I find that approach is more successful for me because I'm able to radiate enthusiasm. I think structuring for me would ruin it. I need to go with my own gut feeling.

FEEDBACK THAT COUNTS

To me, success is when you get feedback from people indicating that you've helped them, because you never really stop. Every day you just keep going, and I don't think you can measure it in monetary rewards. Money opens the doors, that's all. What's more important is how your peers look at you. Do they respect what you say? Do they come to you for advice? Are you recognized? That's success for me.

I feel that I'm successful, but I feel that I need to go further. I want to see my company grow so that there are many other people like me within my company so we are able to reach out to more people and help them. We are really in a business to help companies grow and I'm only one person.

LISTEN AND LEARN

One of the most important factors in achieving success is taking the time to listen and help people—never being too busy for the other person. In helping that other person you'll learn things that will help you. I really believe that.

For example, a gal whom I had not met called me one day and said she had gotten the musical rights to use the song for Mercedes Boy. She wanted to film a commercial for Mercedes, but she didn't have a Mercedes. She called me and said, "Someone said you had a Mercedes and I really want to do this video."

She had thrown the idea to the Mercedes Corporation and they liked it, but they wanted to see a finished video. They were going to film it at the Capitol here in Sacramento and my thought was, "This is a way to promote Sacramento and it's a way for her to promote her business. So, I'll live without the car whenever she needs to borrow it."

I loaned it to her three or four times and it looks like Mercedes is going to buy the commercial. I could have said, "This is a very expensive car." Instead, I said, "Take care of it the way you would your own."

I decided to take that chance. Now I know that I can call this girl and she will find a way to help me with anything I need, because I helped her.

THE LITTLE THINGS THAT COUNT

Staying in touch with people is very important. One of the things that I tell people to do when they meet someone or they are handed that business card is to write on the back of it. Include the things that transpired in the conversation—perhaps the person said he loves boats or he's a golfer. Then drop a line and include something in the note that has to do with his interests.

One of the things I found while working in New York was no matter how big the people are in their companies, they like great sayings and great words of wisdom.

There are presidents of major corporations in New York with whom I've constantly stayed in touch. I'll send a little poem to them and they'll write back to say, "How did you know I needed that?" It's just a way of putting your name out there without asking for anything. It separates you from everybody else, positioning you above your competition. It's that extra mile that you're willing to go that counts.

THE CLIENT BASE

Included among my clients is a company called Starbeam, in Dallas, which manufactures a light that mounts on a truck and throws out one hundred, fifty thousand kilowatts of power that can increase to one million. Right now we have sold to one Coast Guard base, one Navy base and two Army bases.

One Army base that just bought one sent its representative with a purchase order for seven more and is considering an additional five hundred. I have the light in the Air Force testing program right now, which will be very big for us, and I just sent a letter to General Powell of the Joint Chiefs of Staff to look at it for the Army's readiness group. I have a feeling this is going to move really well in a big way.

"The law of averages says when you use the direct mail approach...the fourth time the name is instilled in their memory."

"...I'm able to radiate enthusiasm."

I have another product out of Arizona which is the world's first nickel cadmium battery that is solar re-charged. This comes from a guy who is an inventor. He doesn't have a lot of money. I have another client in Massachusetts who has reams of money, and I put them together. Now the client in Massachusetts is buying out the Arizona company!

The biggest challenge in selling to the government is finding the right people to make the decisions. After you do it awhile you learn who they are and where they are and your name works its way through the system. I'm fairly well known on most of the bases, so when I call for an appointment I will usually be given one.

EXCELLENT REPRESENTATION

To me, business excellence is making sure the products I represent are of the highest quality and that the service of the companies I represent is also of the highest quality. The ethics have to be way up there.

Excerpts from tributes to Robbie Motter from co-workers and business associates:

Dedicated to Robbie Motter
LEAVING

The pleasure has been mine, for I've learned from what you know. And, even as you're leaving, that knowledge will always grow. You're a flower that bloomed in our field, the spring breeze blew your fragrance around, making our success unending, and the magic of achievement abound. I've seen what you've achieved and know you won't stop now, so as you leave us, stand proudly as always and give your final bow.

—By June Jones

CERTIFICATE OF HONOR
To: Ms. Robbie Miracle Worker Motter
In Recognition of Outstanding Services
Awarded By The Office of Property Management
Ms. Robbie Mardi Gras Motter, renowned manipula-
tor of office automation jargon, is hereby acclaimed to be
an honorary member of the Society of Friends from the
Office of Property Management. Cherished for her success
in bringing microcomputers into the FSS wilderness, the
Office of Property Management has decided to re-
dedicate its Xerox 2 microcomputer by renaming it the
"MicroMotter." We, from outside areas, who were privi-
leged to work with Robbie can attest to her noteworthy
contributions, always characterized by her wit, charisma,
intelligence and professionalism.
Bill Foote
Director, Office of Property Management
Stanley M. Duda
Director, Utilization Division
Michael D. Driessen
Understudy to the above

A NOTE
There are people whose medium is Life itself and
who express the inexpressible without brush, pencil,
chisel or guitar. They neither paint nor dance. Their
medium is Being. Whatever their hand touches has
increased Life. They see and don't have to draw. They are
the artists of being alive. You Robbie are one of these.
Please thank all your family for their kindness.
—Sue Bruns

> **Robbie Motter**
> **Contacts Unlimited Inc.**
> **1110 Oakridge Dr**
> **Roseville, CA 95661**
> **Business: 916-784-8366**
> **Message: 916-348-2068**

Ron Patterson and Darlene Shaffer-Patterson are co-owners of John Robert Powers, a modeling school and agency. Prior to founding JRP in Sacramento, Mr. Patterson managed public relations and special events for a large department store chain. Ms. Shaffer-Patterson formerly was a manager of Gloria Marshall's Figure Salons and various modeling schools and agencies.

A s they look around their new posh facility in Rancho Cordova, Ron Patterson and Darlene Shaffer-Patterson realize they have many reasons to celebrate. In just a little more than a year, their John Robert Powers modeling agency had completely outgrown its three-thousand-square-foot Citrus Heights location. Subsequently, they have recently moved to an expansive seventeen-thousand-square-foot facility.

The space is not all that is expanding.

What began as a modeling school and talent agency has also become a broadcast school, a beauty salon and a photography school. There are even plans in the works to include an upscale deli in the building.

How have Ron and Darlene accomplished this feat? Very simply, promotion. They have developed extremely successful marketing techniques, attracting many of Sacramento's young people to their door.

Both are extremely active in local charities, contributing generous amounts of time and money to causes such as the March of Dimes. Their generosity in the community has earned them several awards.

It has not been an easy climb to success for these two enterprising individuals, though. They have endured business failure, financial ruin and their own divorce. Fortunately, they are optimists and believe that the lessons they have learned along the way, though sometimes harsh, have made them stronger and better prepared to handle the prosperity they now enjoy.

Ron and Darlene have no plans to stop with the Rancho Cordova operation, by the way. Now that they have found their entrepreneurial niche, they have plans to expand their operation throughout Northern California.

"In a corporate environment, creativity and originality are not always rewarded."

"Everything we had

worked for and saved

was taken from us. We

had to file bankruptcy

ourselves in 1984."

Author's Note: *Image is king in the modeling and talent business. Therefore I was pleasantly surprised at the candidness with which Ron and Darlene spoke of their personal lives, with no holds barred. An enjoyable interview.*

RON: If I had it to do over, I would have chosen the path of an entrepreneur much sooner. I wanted to do it when I was nineteen, but I was afraid. I thought you needed to work for someone—for a corporation that would take care of you. Had I started on my own then, I would have passed through the trial and error stage much sooner—a painful but necessary aspect of new business ownership.

I started as a janitor for a large department store chain in the early 1970s and was promoted up the ranks to merchandiser, buyer and eventually transferred to a district staff position in Sacramento. At the top end of my job, I had a budget of about $13 million dollars and seventy employees. From there I was promoted to public relations and special events for the company—a position that really helped me to acquire the media savvy I use in my own business today.

Although I was progressing, there always seemed to be something missing. In a corporate environment creativity and originality are not always rewarded.

When I left the company, I truly felt like I had been let out of prison.

BANKRUPTCY—THE OPTIMIST'S LEARNING EXPERIENCE
Working for somebody and then starting a business for yourself is tough. Before Darlene and I started with John Robert Powers, we had some failures—the trial and error part of venturing into your own business.

While I was still at the department store in 1983, we started a fitness program called A Woman's Touch, which did quite well. At the same time though, I got into a partnership for a downtown nightclub that turned out to be disastrous. It started out to be fairly successful, but I realized early on that a night club was not going to help me meet my goals of wealth and comfort, so I sold my share to my partners.

A year later they went bankrupt. Since my name was on the original agreements, I was held responsible for payment. Even though I had sold my share of the business, our bank accounts were frozen and our wages were attached. Everything we had worked for and saved was taken from us. We had to file bankruptcy ourselves in 1984.

Although devastating, it was the educational event of my career.

Initially I thought, "I'm going to be in this trap all my life," but fortunately I am an incurable positive thinker. We cut back to spending ten dollars a week on groceries, instituted a plan and started saving again.

No amount of formal education could ever have taught me what the bankruptcy did. I almost believe that the way to success is through bankruptcy.

The biggest obstacle we faced in the purchase of our JRP franchise was getting started. We couldn't find anyone who would give us any help. We had been bankrupt—we didn't have any believers. We had to sacrifice personally to do it, and interestingly, not a day goes by now, that people don't offer us money to open another one.

We have a line of credit at the bank that is unlimited. We're opening a branch in Stockton for which we have already signed a lease. We have gone from Darlene, a receptionist, and me, to currently forty-eight employees. We will be hiring another forty within the next month.

It just takes confidence in yourself and positive thinking to carry your plans through.

"I became a great motivational speaker for the church..."

A SPIRITUAL FOUNDATION

I developed confidence in myself as a child. A lot of it goes back to my training in church activities. I can't remember a time when I wasn't knocking on people's doors, and I learned the ability to talk with people at an early age. The religion made me realize the knack I had to persuade people. I broke all records for magazine and book placements. I gave speeches in Candlestick Park and at Dodger Stadium when I was fifteen. I became a great motivational speaker for the church and one day, when I was in my 20s, I realized—"Hey, I've got talent!" That talent has helped me throughout my career.

I met and married Darlene in the church. We each

"If you want to enjoy a

successful business,

become involved in

and get to know your

community."

brought our impoverished childhoods and dreams of a great future to our missionary work in the church.

DARLENE: My drive came from my parents never doing anything with their lives. I was born in Camden City, New Jersey and moved to New Orleans when I was nine. I came from a very poor family. My father died when I was young, and my mother was a waitress all of her life. She became involved in the church because of her insecurity, I think. I was very shy as a child, but I was still able to place books door to door. It made me a good salesperson, gave me confidence, and it especially helped me with rejection. When I had the belief in my mind that God was guiding me, it was easy to overcome my shyness.

The church also was crucial to the development of my work ethic. We were not allowed to stay home on Saturdays and watch cartoons. Instead, we were out working. We were always involved in some activity, and I continue to work that way today.

When we were married, Ron was a janitor and I cleaned houses. I really wanted to improve myself—to speak, look and feel better about myself—so I started taking modeling classes. The church did not approve of my modeling, and that's when I left.

RON: I was born on an Indian reservation near Farmington, New Mexico, the ninth of thirteen children. We were so poor that we lived in a home with a dirt floor for my first four years. The next four years were spent in a tent by the river with no flooring or plumbing.

I finally started school at age eight, when we moved to town. There, the same teacher taught first through eighth grades. Her name was Mrs. Lancaster and she taught me for six years. She was a very influential person in my life, helping me develop an appreciation for reading. She would also praise me by saying things like "You're going to be a president."

Maybe she told all of the kids that, I don't know, but at least she told me and I felt a lot of self-worth. She believed in me and gave me positive reinforcement, making me believe that I was somebody.

PERSPECTIVES ON SUCCESS
FROM RON PATTERSON & DARLENE SHAFFER-PATTERSON

- Corporate incarceration
- Bankruptcy opens door
- Church instills values
- Model and talent search
- Getting the phone to ring
- Correcting imperfections

"Don't waste your money advertising. Advertise with a promotion."

BENEVOLENT RETURNS

One philosophy of the church I have retained is that giving is a mandate. I believe it is one of the laws of nature—and of running a successful business. Charity comes back immediately. For example, we were recently at a function where we were given leadership awards from the March of Dimes. After the award ceremony, I had five people approach me about their sons or daughters getting into modeling.

We are all over the community. All you need are ten people here, ten people there, and pretty soon your phones are ringing. Involving yourself with good causes is definitely good business.

The people I have met through the March of Dimes, for instance, have an allegiance to me when they think about where to send their children for the sort of training we offer.

If you want to enjoy a successful business, become involved in and get to know your community. Be involved with charity, give to your community and it all comes back. That is ninety percent of my marketing plan—and marketing is ninety-five percent of maintaining a successful business.

REWARDING PROMOTIONS

You could have a palace here but if no one is aware of it, who cares? The most important aspect of successful marketing is promotion. Don't waste your money advertising.

Advertise with a promotion.

For example, we don't write an ad that says, "Come to JRP and let us make you a model." I might get two calls from that. For the same amount of money I can say, "Next month we're sponsoring a big event at the Performing Arts Center at Sacramento High School to raise money

"I have a media guide

and I stay in touch,

taking people to lunch,

sending them notes

and press releases."

for the Center. We're looking for singers, dancers and actors. In addition, Motown and ICM record companies will be here to look at some talent for a video."

For a promotion like this, we'll have over fifteen hundred people audition. But I can take that same amount of money and say, "Come to JRP school of modeling," and get two calls if I'm lucky.

I do a promotion a month. Right now I have events planned monthly for the next year.

We're doing a children's talent and model search. We will send a child to the set of Sesame Street in New York. That will be a big one.

Also planned is a big model and talent search in conjunction with the opening of the film, *Wizard,* and a holiday show just for children.

As a major sponsor of Mace's restaurant and the Mace's Spring Ball—a showcase of local talent—another big audition of singers, dancers and actors will be held.

Also in spring, we will do a Hispanic model search. Last year we had over six hundred Hispanic entrants, indicating a hot market.

Our 4th Annual Teen Model Search will be here in August.

We have also started a program called *Teen Talk.* Joan Engles of KJAY radio hosts it and I sponsor it. We just visited our first school—Grant High. We auditioned about one hundred students to pick a panel, then the show was taped in the school auditorium with the selected panel, its members talking about any subject they chose.

We will be doing this with eight high school and elementary schools a month. It doesn't cost me anything, and it's giving to both the community and the kids. Those kids at Grant talked about a lot of subjects, and we developed some real friends.

Finally, we have the annual Cover Girl contest. We pick a top face, a new face, to send to New York to the IMTA, the International Model and Talent Association.

To punch up our mailing list, we acquired seven thousand new names by handing out fliers for a drawing for free lessons at the opening Kings' game this season. All it cost me was the printing.

You see, we know the community, and we cover all aspects of it with promotion and participation—not merely advertising.

Because I know the media, I am able to get the word out about our impending events. I send out press releases every week, maintaining a good rapport with area radio and television stations, as well as with newspapers. I have a media guide and I stay in touch, taking people to lunch, sending them notes and press releases. They may not use one today, but they will do something different next month.

You've got to get out there, make people notice you differently. I always thought that if I had a gas station, I would have the attendants wear roller skates because it would make people notice them.

Whatever you're doing you must create a gimmick to attract attention. You can get involved with charity, develop your own fund raiser so people know who you are. You just have to be a bit creative to orchestrate the right promotion for your business.

"For someone with the dream of owning his own business, I say do your homework."

DISCOVERIES ARE FEW IN THE TALENT GAME

The modeling industry has changed dramatically over the years as there is no longer a "typical" model type. Everybody alive has something that an advertiser can use for a commercial or to show his product, but people just don't realize it. Two of our top models were formerly our electrician and our postman.

In our day and age you're not going to become another Lana Turner by sitting on a stool at a drugstore lunch counter and being discovered. There are too many acting schools churning out too many talented actors for scouts to pull from. They don't have to "discover" someone and teach him or her because there are millions of people learning to act and model and becoming skilled at it. The business has changed. Anyone who thinks he or she is going to be "discovered" is living in the past.

We see agents from Los Angeles and New York all the time. They come here, and they go to every school in the country. They don't have to do what they used to do, since the burden is on our shoulders now to find the talent.

If we get any of our people on television, they receive thirty to fifty thousand dollars each, and we're paid fifteen percent of that. It's worth finding these people and training them. I can tell if they have physical potential, but what's more important than that is what is inside them. They have to be go-getters with a positive

"To me success is

when you overcome a

lot of the things that

stand in your way,

when your view of

life's challenges is that

no matter how difficult

it is, you know you will

be able to work around

any obstacle standing

in your way."

feeling about themselves, and surprisingly, most attractive people don't have that.

HANDLING CLIENTS WITH CARE

We strive hard to take good care of our clients. An important aspect of success in this heavy referral business is keeping your clients happy. We are unique because of the passion Darlene and I have for the business, along with our commitment to excellence. I want to give these people something, to see my kids on television and in the movies. I want to see them in the newspaper, and I don't quit until I know we are giving them quality. That's the difference between John Robert Powers and its competitors.

DARLENE: Our clients are from all walks of life. There are lots of people out there who really have a dream. What we do is try to make that dream happen, whether they want to sing or dance, to be in the theater or do television commercials. I always ask clients to define their goal up front to find out what they really want. If they say they want to be a model—What type of model? Where do you see yourself? What do you want to do? The more you define a goal, the greater chance you have of reaching it.

We don't try to change the person, but to correct their imperfections, and change the things about themselves they don't like. If they are overweight, they can lose; if they hate their nose, they can have it fixed. If they don't have enough confidence, we can help them lose their fears, and that way gain self-confidence.

DIFFERING MANAGEMENT STYLES DEFINE THE BALANCE

RON: The clients really love working with our staff. They think we're easy to work with, and we are accommodating as we spend a lot of time on motivating our employees. Through training, meetings, recognition and meaningful responsibility, we have provided a good environment for them.

DARLENE: It has been said that you can't work with friends and family, but I find that to be untrue. As sales director, I am working with my ex-husband, and I have friends who work here too. We all have a lot of respect for each other.

If I am experiencing problems with an employee, my big heart tends to want to see them improve. Employees all have their personal lives, and it's hard to say, "Leave these problems outside the door when you walk in here." When I know there's something bothering a person, I have to look inside and find out what is wrong. Once the employee confides in me, I am more understanding, and I want to work with that individual so he or she is not afraid of being fired. I would much rather work everything out with the person.

Our employees have to feel that their job is not on the line simply because they tell me something I don't like. That helps me. I like those kinds of evaluations. Who else evaluates you when you're the boss? You have to get the feedback from your people as it helps you become a better person.

RON: We roll up our sleeves, and we do everything we ask our people to do right here with them side by side. We do a lot of rewarding because I don't want our employees to get lip service from me. They benefit directly from the money that comes in the door. We have a great bonus system where I pay for ideas. If one of my employees comes up with a promotional idea, we pay him or her five hundred dollars. We pay them daily if they reach certain goals, and now we're getting ready to set up a profit sharing plan. I think most of the problems we encounter in our business are people problems. I try to work through problems with my employees, but this business is my baby, so when it comes down to the wire, I am not going to let anyone hurt my baby.

"I want to give these people something, to see my kids on television and in the movies."

THE SUCCESSFUL DEFINITION

I think what really makes me successful today is that I operate every day as though the company is going to be taken away from me—almost as though I don't deserve it. I'm afraid it's going to go away so I work very hard every day. I will never have that totally relaxed feeling of, "I've made it." I am sure that goes back to my poverty as a child.

I also read constantly—business magazines, business books—all the new ones that come out like *How to Swim With the Sharks Without Being Eaten Alive*. I apply principles of those success oriented books to my business.

I think my number one secret to success, though, is positive thinking, followed by persistence.

For someone with the dream of owning his own business, I say do your homework. You need to have a

"Once the employee confides in me, I am more understanding, and I want to work with that individual so he or she is not afraid of being fired."

plan, and it has to be in writing. Don't just open your doors and wait for your phone to ring. If I did that we'd be broke. Get involved in your community—*make* your phone ring. Become your own biggest salesperson—you've got to live and breathe your business.

Darlene and I had a commitment in the beginning. We had to make 65 phone calls each, every day, to reach out and touch someone. Even today with all our admissions, we have a plan that we have to reach out and touch so many people. Set goals. If you don't have them, you won't get anywhere.

Sacramento is an exploding market, and we're only in our infancy. If you can't see that, you had better take a long hard look at your techniques.

DARLENE: To me success is when you overcome a lot of the things that stand in your way, when your view of life's challenges is that no matter how difficult it is, you know you will be able to work around any obstacle standing in your way. I feel that everything in life is temporary anyway.

Money has very little to do with success. I think if you do something well the money will follow.

I know a lot of people who are successful in terms of material things, with a beautiful home, beautiful cars, the whole works. These people are very unhappy. Personally, I'd rather keep things simple.

RON: My definition of success has changed. I used to equate it with money and now I equate it with a balanced life—that involves my personal life, as well as my business life. I need more now than just money and the business. You've got to have a personal life that includes sharing with someone because when you go home by yourself, you're going home to yourself. I don't care how fancy the house is—you're alone. I want a good balance there, and it's hard sometimes, but I'm working toward it. It's one of my priorities to include another person in my life, ensuring that I have a quality existence.

As with every other goal in life, you have to have the vision in your mind. Everything that has happened, I created first in my mind, even the personal success. I start focusing on something that I want and I get it. I don't know what that power is called, but I've developed it, and I think we all have it, we just don't know it. It's awesome.

Ron Patterson
Darlene Shaffer-Patterson
John Robert Powers Modeling School and Agency
10680 White Rock Road
Rancho Cordova, CA 95670
916-852-2100

Jim Pelley

Jim Pelley
*is Director of Every-
thing and Emperor for
Marketing and
Product Development
for a company he
founded called
Laughter Works. For-
merly a stand-up
comedian and comedy
writer, Pelley is a
popular speaker who
gets bucks for yucks by
speaking to more than
seventeen thousand
seminar attendees a
year at various
locations throughout
the United States,
Canada, and Japan.*

I wake up to the alarm that beeps, grab a cup of coffee from the pot that beeps, enter the car that beeps, work on a computer that beeps, take money from the automatic teller machine that beeps and talk to the answering machine that beeps. No wonder I'm a bleeping maniac by the end of the day!"

That's Jim Pelley, humor guru, parodying the American lifestyle and getting his seminar audience to warm up to him. He has an important message to deliver, after they're in the right mood.

"You know, a recent poll stated that the number one fear among people is public speaking, and the number six fear is death," Pelley tells his audience with mock sincerity. "So the next time somebody commits a violent crime, the police should put him on the lecture circuit."

A highly polished speaker, Pelley thrives on helping people overcome daily stress by laughing at themselves. He delivers his humor technology to such organizations as AT&T, Pacific Gas & Electric, Embassy Suites, All Nippon Airlines, United States Air Force, IBM, Pacific Bell, Sutter Hospitals, Price Waterhouse, Sacramento Unified School District and the United States Forest Service.

He offers workshops, retreats, seminars and private consultation. Two of Laughter Works' most requested seminars are: *Laughter—There is Nothing Funny About the Way it SELLS* and *MBHA...Management By Horsing Around*.

Pelley's working tips on bringing humor into the workplace have been photocopied and disseminated throughout corporate America almost as much as Gary Larson's Far Side cartoons.

Some examples: When you are stumped for a solution to a problem, grab your hand-held megaphone and shout, "It's idea solution time!" Gather the group together for a five-minute brainstorming session and let each

"I developed the unique talent of making people laugh, and that got me through a lot of the pain."

"...projections indicated the industry would generate $90 billion in revenue by the year 2000."

person contribute half a dozen spontaneous ideas with no critique. It's quick, simple and fun, and it usually triggers something new and creative.

Or, when faced with chronic complainers in the office, require that everyone sing his or her complaints.

How about sprinkling tidbits of wisdom throughout memoranda. One of Pelley's favorites is, "No problem is so big that it can't be solved by a miracle."

When collecting bills, Pelley offers this solution: "Instead of calling your lawyer when someone won't pay you, first try sending a bill that's two feet long. You'll certainly grab their attention."

Author's Note: Jim Pelley invited me to his home for the interview. He had just returned from a speaking engagement and was visibly tired and seemed a little down. I wondered if he had enough left in him to do the interview, so I asked him how he was feeling. He smiled and immediately did two minutes of upbeat comedy.

Looking back at my youth, humor and speaking have always been prominent parts of my personality. My knack for entertaining began when I was a young boy growing up in Napa. For starters, I was dyslexic, color blind and rather clumsy at sports. Those traits alone were enough to make grade school a living hell. Fortunately, I developed the unique talent of making people laugh, and that got me through a lot of the pain.

My fifth and sixth grade teacher helped a lot back then, too. Bob Crossley was the kindest, gentlest man I ever met. I remember talking to him in the afternoons at his desk while he graded papers, or at his home on the weekends while he changed the oil in his car. He was very supportive of me. Unequivocally, what I'm doing now, I do for Bob, who died when he was only thirty-eight years old.

My mother was also a great inspiration. In fact both of my parents gave me unconditional love and support. I am very fortunate that I had that foundation upon which to build my life.

MY LIFE AS A STAND-UP COMIC

I haven't always been a speaker and humor coach. I have done everything from commodities trading to performing as the opening act for Father Guido Sarducci! When I was a freshman in college, Don Novello, who plays the Father, was coming to do a benefit for the Napa Valley College. The president of the college, who was also a good friend of mine, asked my friend, Mike—also a funny guy—and me to open the show.

So we did it.

Part of the skit was a take-off on the Julio Iglesias/ Willie Nelson song, *To All The Girls I've Loved Before*. It was taped by Showtime and ended up on *Saturday Night Live* and *The Tonight Show*—instantly our comedy hit the entire grand comedy circuit!

ENJOYABLE ENDEAVORS

Upon graduating from Sacramento State with a degree in Communication Studies, the first thing I did was to sit down and make a list of what I love to do. It was a very small list. It basically consisted of traveling and speaking, two very enjoyable endeavors. I had one big question: why would anyone pay me for this?

I didn't do a lot of market research. I knew three statistics. I knew what other speakers were getting paid, that trade associations were spending $500 million a year in Sacramento on meetings, and that projections indicated the industry would generate $90 billion in revenue by the year 2000.

I actually came to Sacramento as a business major. At that time I was involved very actively in the commodities market. Business school turned me off because there was such a great emphasis on teaching by case study, by the book, rather than by real life application. As an entrepreneur, I wasn't going to learn anything by studying the history of an IBM or a Hewlett-Packard. It wasn't relevant, and it drove me nuts, so I changed to communication studies.

CONFESSIONS OF A CLOSET CASE

Actually, Laughter Works started in a closet. It really did. After graduation I lived in a one bedroom apart-

"I have done everything from commodities trading to performing as the opening act for Father Guido Sarducci!"

"...the skit ended up on

Saturday Night Live

and the Tonight Show

– instantly our comedy

hit the entire grand

comedy circuit!"

ment, so I took the doors off one of the closets and put my desk in it. Later, I added a file cabinet and a Macintosh.

In starting out I think the single biggest obstacle was marketing myself. In the speaking business you get most of your business by referrals from people who've heard you speak. I started off doing the lunch club circuit. I spoke at the Rotaries and the Kiwanis for free and, little by little, began to get referrals. We are now at the point that we average two referral calls a day.

PERSPECTIVES ON SUCCESS FROM JIM PELLEY
- Saturday Night Live
- Creativity leads the way
- Father Guido Sarducci
- The office clown
- Telling jokes
- Generic humor

HUMOR CAUSES MORE THAN MERE LAUGHTER
There's nothing more exciting for me, as a speaker, than to change the attitudes of an audience. I try to teach people that humor isn't a trivial part of life, instead it's an integral part of personal happiness. People need to take humor seriously.

I can't think of a single person in the world who doesn't want to be happier and more fulfilled. Self-actualization, growth, self-esteem—they all start with a good sense of humor. That's what I'm giving people.

CREATIVITY COMES IN MANY FORMS
Creativity is the key to the success in any business, not capitalization or long hours or good accounting. It isn't just your creativity, but the creativity of your advisers. So I always, always, always consult the expert. I did a lot of research on the law firm that I chose because I wanted to find the right one for me. My attorney's great. He doesn't say, "Oh, we're sunk." Instead, he goes out there and says, "We're gonna kick butt."

I have my newsletters published by The Newsletter Company, and my publicist is the best. She's written for Reader's Digest, Family Circle, Working Woman—you name it, she has done it.

These people don't tell me what I can't do. I tell them where I want to go, and they tell me the best way to get there. They are the kind of people I want on my side.

KNOWING WHEN TO BE IN CONTROL

Loss of control is a reality of business, though it's difficult for most entrepreneurs to handle. Think of your business as a team of horses. You're driving in a wagon, and you're controlling the reins of four teams of horses. You need to realize you can't hold all those reins yourself, so in effect, what you need to do is have someone on your side to take a pair of horses. These people need direction from you, when to go to the right or when to go to the left, and you need to know when to give up control.

Another crucial step is knowing the exact moment to plug in those people. If you do it too soon you're going to cause a serious capital drain, and if you do it too late, you lose your business.

PASSION

In order to excel in business, I truly believe you must have a passion for it, a passion to be the best at what you do. You'll be there. You'll do the job and do it on time. If you have the passion, you will go out of your way, not only to do the job well, but to do it in an excellent manner, to the very best of your ability.

BLANKETS AS THEY RELATE TO STRESS

I love this job. The only thing I hate is the number of hours it takes. I tell people, the nice thing about owning your own business is you can choose which seventy hours you want to work during the week! Believe me, a seventy-hour workweek can be stressful.

I have found some very practical ways to relieve stress. For example, ask yourself how your favorite comedian would deal with whatever stresses you, or find a new way to approach what's stressful. If getting out of bed in the morning when your alarm goes off is stressful for you, try something different. Don't use an alarm clock, instead put a timer on the stereo. Try waking up to someone kissing you.

Stress is really caused by our perception of an event. The trick is to learn to see things not as they are, but as they could be by using creative problem solving for stress reduction. In fact, the two are almost synonymous; both are powerful tools.

"Actually, Laughter Works started in a closet."

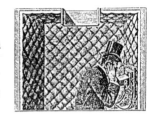

"People need to take

humor seriously."

RED NOSES ARE NOT A REQUIREMENT

People come in expecting us to teach them how to tell jokes, but they find out fairly quickly that's not what Laughter Works is all about. We don't talk about humor as a way to be funny, although it is a by-product. We don't teach people how to be office clowns. We teach them some appropriate and positive techniques—skills and tools—that are practical and truly applicable in the workplace.

You go to a normal stress reduction seminar and you hear that you need to work out for fifteen minutes a day at least three days a week. The first thing people say is, "I can't do that. I don't have the time." What they hear from us is, "Hey, you can reduce stress right where you are at the moment." When you're in your car and you're stressed out and you need to laugh a little bit, pop in a Smothers Brothers' tape. Find five funny things in the environment around you. All of the things we come up with encourage our clients to think.

MIND OVER MONEY

Another important concept is emotional income. I say that life is too short to park your own car, for instance. It costs $4 to park in the garage down here. It costs an extra $5 to have a valet. Big deal. Don't let $5 be a problem when a valet will take so much added pressure off your life.

You only have so much real income, but each one of us also has only so much emotional income. You have to save and adjust your emotional budget so that the little things like parking your car won't send you into emotional bankruptcy. Spend the extra five dollars if the valet makes you feel good.

THANKS FOR THE REJECTION

We did a program for the sales force at the Embassy Suites Hotel in Los Angeles. Cold calls were one of their number one fears. Our solution was to have the salespeople try a new method when faced with rejection. We had the people call the negative responding companies and thank them. Not for going with someone else, but for their time, for listening to the presentation.

Even though you don't choose a particular product it's hard to say why. The firms might not have chosen the Embassy Suites because they needed a better location.

That doesn't mean they won't consider it in the

future. If you call them up and say, "I want to thank you for considering us, maybe we can work with you again in the future," they're likely to call you again.

I've received a lot of positive feedback on that approach. There's a lot of tension when you call to thank someone for not engaging your product. Humor will come out of it just naturally—you'll end up joking with the guy. It's a technique that works. In fact, Laughter Works is built on thank-yous.

YOU DON'T HAVE TO BE HENNY YOUNGMAN

I think there is a lot to be learned by spending the day with a professional in almost any facet of life in which you are interested. For example, anyone who has ever played football would no doubt improve his game by spending a day with a professional football coach. He may not leave with the skill of Joe Montana, but he would improve.

People come to me and say, "I can't tell a joke." Well, as a humor consultant, the first thing I tell them is, "Don't tell jokes. If you're not good at it don't do it."

Joke telling is only one of two dozen forms of humor. People who can't tell jokes should use other techniques—humorous slides in a presentation for example, or use humorous quotes.

One of the things we do in our workshops is to have people take an embarrassing situation and explain it to the class. We talk about some generic humor rules and apply them to various situations. There's just no such thing as someone who doesn't have a sense of humor— only people who have chosen not to develop it.

Jim Pelley
Laughter Works
222 Selby Ranch Road, Suite 4
Sacramento, CA 95864-5832
916-484-7988

"...the nice thing about owning your own business is you can choose which seventy hours you want to work during the week!"

Steven D. Pomerantz *is a licensed family therapist, who helps clients handle relationships, family, personal growth and problems at work.*
Mr. Pomerantz has been a member of the adjunct faculty of the University of San Francisco for more than six years, teaching several courses in the bachelor's and master's programs in organizational behavior and development. He is the former president of the Sacramento Valley Chapter of the California Association of Marriage and Family Therapists, the American Society for Training and Development (ASTD) and Toastmasters International.

"**Y**ou are members of a space crew originally scheduled to rendezvous with a mother ship on the lighted surface of the moon. Due to mechanical difficulties, however, your ship was forced to land at a spot some two hundred earth miles from the rendezvous point.

"My biggest fear was

public speaking."

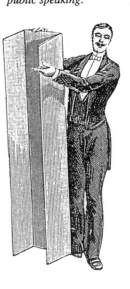

"During re-entry and landing, much of the equipment aboard was damaged and, since survival depends on reaching the mother ship, the most critical items available must be chosen for the two-hundred-mile trip."

The men and women sitting in the conference room study their sheets of paper. Soon they will compare choices and discuss their implications. Then they will be asked to re-evaluate their original decisions after hearing what others think.

Although resembling a NASA training session, this is actually a seminar on leadership and motivation being conducted by Steve Pomerantz. Through scenarios such as the NASA Moon Survival Task, Steve illustrates the natural development of work groups. Participants learn how leaders are selected and how to recognize different leadership types.

The result is a clearer understanding of one's role in helping a work group to achieve its maximum potential for effective functioning, particularly where creative endeavors are involved.

Pomerantz has conducted more than four hundred and fifty seminars for over ten thousand participants on subjects including leadership and motivation, time management, stress management, management by objectives, effective communication, problem solving and conflict resolution.

"They were eloquent,

dramatic and

dynamic—everything I

wasn't."

Author's Note: *Steve and I sipped honey-laced herb tea at his office off Bradshaw while engaging in pre-interview chit-chat. We quickly established a warm and friendly rapport. I thought, "I would feel safe telling all my secrets to this guy." Apparently, he felt the same way. I switched on the recorder and, to my delight, he revealed his innermost secrets of success.*

I think one of the most important things you must do in life is confront your fears. My biggest fear was public speaking. Today, I earn a good part of my living through public speaking and giving seminars. But I haven't always been an effective speaker—in fact, quite the opposite.

All through school I was very shy. The first time I had to give an oral presentation I was in fifth grade. It was the first day of class and the teacher made us write a paragraph about what we did during the summer. After we all wrote our paragraphs, the teacher said, "Now everybody's going to get up in front of the class and give their report." When my turn came, I was so intimidated and embarrassed, I just couldn't do it. The desks had lids on them and I was actually to the point where I lifted the lid to hide my head in shame.

A NEW OUTLOOK

I didn't face my fear of speaking until I had finished college and was working. I found myself moving into leadership positions. When you're in a leadership position, you have to do some kind of speaking in front of groups. I muddled my way through when I was a department head in Placer County, until one day at lunch a commissioner, whom I trusted and got along well with, approached me.

He said, "Did you ever think of going to Toastmasters?"

I said, "Yes, I have. I've thought about it, but never really found the time."

He told me to find the time.

"You do okay now," he said, "but you could do much better."

A couple of months later I made the time and I went. I was terrified, with all the fears from fifth grade coming back.

It was a group of people who met for breakfast, seated in a "U" shape. Every Toastmaster club has basically the same procedure that they go through—each person gets up and speaks. They started going through it, and in my perception, every person who spoke was a polished, professional speaker. They were eloquent, dramatic and dynamic—everything I wasn't.

At the end of the meeting they asked me if I would like to say something. I said, "Well, I enjoyed being here, and I'll probably join." Still I was just terrified!

AH, DON'T DO IT ANYMORE

So I joined, knowing I had to force myself to do this. For the first three months I could hardly eat breakfast. Everybody had some speaking part during the meeting, even if it was just to introduce somebody else.

Slowly, I started speaking; in fact, I had the job of the "ah" counter. An "ah" counter is someone who sits there and counts your "ahs" as you speak. At the end, you give the "ah" report. Joe had six "ahs." Mary had twenty-three "ahs." Whoever has the most "ahs" gets the "ah" award, which is a tongue depressor on a string you must wear at the next meeting. It's very reinforcing as far as making you aware of your "ahs," and controlling them.

Anyhow, it was my turn to give the "ah" report. I used so many "ahs" in giving the "ah" report that I won the "ah" award. It was the first time that anyone giving the "ah" report had won the award!

I had to confront my weaknesses and fears in a semi-serious, semi-humorous fashion through the Toastmasters, and about the fourth month I started to give good presentations. I even represented our chapter in a contest and won!

One of my highest recommendations to anyone is to go to Toastmasters. It's wonderful! I recommend it to many of my clients, and I tell them not to pay me as much for therapy and instead go to Toastmasters. It's cheaper and you'll get much more out of it faster.

"...I used so many 'ahs' in giving the 'ah' report that I won the 'ah' award."

"I want you to get up

here in front of the

group...then I want

everybody in the

audience to boo her."

THE CONFIDENCE TO CHANGE

It became clear to me that I was getting bored with my job with Placer County. It looked like doing some family therapy and individual therapy, training programs and doing some consulting with organizations would be more rewarding.

As a county department head, I had hired some consultants and had an idea of what it was about. I had gone to many training seminars and felt impressed with the people who were conducting them, and always said to myself, "Well, I'd like to do that." Now that I had gotten over my fear of speaking, I felt I was ready.

PERSPECTIVES ON SUCCESS FROM STEVE POMERANTZ

- Confronting fears
- Tongue depressor cures "ahs"
- Diversity provides balance
- Conrad Hilton's story
- Persistence pays off
- Only the strong can be gentle

THE ROAR OF THE CROWD

In one of my first seminars, I was able to help someone else over their fear of speaking. I conducted a training seminar for CalTrans managers several years ago on public speaking, and there were some managers who were terrified of speaking. I required them to get up and give presentations.

There was a woman that talked very softly and I knew what she was feeling as I had been through it myself. She had to get over that worst fear. I asked her what her worst fear was about speaking, but she said she didn't know. I was sure she knew, but she was so nervous about it that she couldn't possibly let it enter her conscious awareness. I told her that her worst fear was that everybody would think that she was the worst speaker and boo her.

I said, "I want you to get up here in front of the group and just stand there, then I want everybody in the audience to boo her. Boo the hell out of her, and I want you to just stay there and look every person in the eye as they're booing you." She did this for about three minutes. There were about fifty people and they really got into it. Some of them were even throwing paper!

The next day in class she gave the best presentation.

She was dynamic and she was forceful.

Afterwards we asked her about the whole experience and she said the booing did it, because she went home and realized she survived the most embarrassing situation she had ever faced in her whole life. Nothing could have been worse, so she just said, "The hell with it, I can do whatever I want!"

EDUCATIONAL PURSUITS

After receiving my bachelor's degree from Pacific University in Oregon, I pursued psychology because I really enjoyed learning about myself and other people. Having been a person who was shy, it was important for me to learn about how other people operate because I always had in my mind the impression that they were doing much better than I was. It was comforting to find out that they were struggling just as much as I was.

It was 1969 when I graduated, and I served two years as director of a drug abuse and suicide prevention center.

This center was located in Chico, and I started working on my master's degree while I was there. I took one or two courses a semester during that two-year period as well as worked full time.

After I completed my master's, I got a job as a field supervisor in a social service program in Butte County and worked there for a couple of years. Then I moved on to Placer County, where I worked as the director of the Human Relations Department for nearly six years.

Earning the balance of my marriage-family-child counseling license required an internship, so I volunteered at a social service agency at night, and I earned hours that way.

Eight years ago, I made a promise to myself that I would be enrolled in a doctoral program by the time I was forty. I enrolled, and will complete my doctorate in Counseling Psychology, and Organization and Leadership at the University of San Francisco in 1991.

DON'T GIVE UP

I went into business for myself in 1981, but it took me two more years to get my MFC license.

Throughout my life I've learned that patience with myself and perseverance pays off. As I've found talking to people who are successful, most of them didn't make it the first time. It's a matter of just plugging away. That's a

"I went out and did all the right things to market myself and the immediate response was nil."

"I enjoy the balance

that the diversity of my

work brings."

big lesson I've learned.

In reading different books about people, that lesson has been reinforced. For instance, one time when I stayed in a Hilton hotel, I read a book Conrad Hilton had written about himself. This guy was the biggest failure when you start counting all the things he had attempted. Seventy percent of the time he screwed up, but he kept plugging along. Of course, now Hilton hotels are famous, and this guy has been the reason why, but in his book he says he just persevered and didn't let failure get in the way of being successful.

PERSISTENCE PAYS OFF

The first year after I left Placer County, my salary went from over thirty thousand dollars a year to three thousand dollars. That was a shock to the system as well as to the pocketbook.

I went out and did all the right things to market myself, and the immediate response was nil.

I sent out brochures, and I went around to all the service clubs and gave my humorous speech that I'd won with. It was a promotional thing. I would entertain them at their breakfast or lunch meeting, or whatever.

When I started my business, I focused on getting contracts with the state and sending in as many bids as possible. In some cases I was low bidder, but they didn't know me and they rejected my bid anyway. Even though I could have filed an appeal, I probably would have made a lot of enemies.

Instead, I went down to the two state organizations that were sending out a lot of contracts. I walked in and said, "Hi, I'm Steve Pomerantz, and I'm the guy who's been sending in all these bids that you've been turning down, and I'd like to talk to somebody."

So, they had me talk to different managers. I told them I had left a very lucrative county department head position to go into private practice. I said, "I'm taking this seriously, and you're going to see my name until you're sick of it, even if I have to plant myself here every day until you give me a contract!" I was angry, frustrated, and I was sure I made them angry.

Fortunately, it had the reverse effect. They thought I had so much gall that maybe they should give me a contract just to see what I could do. Two months later I finally received a contract. Persistence paid off!

DIVERSITY PROVIDES THE BALANCE

Today, I have a diversified business. I do counseling, and I see individual clients, couples and some families. I also consult with organizations, doing training programs, leadership, motivation, problem solving, time management and stress management. My programs last anywhere from a half day to two or three days. I'll design programs to specifically meet the needs of the organization with which I am working.

Let's say there is an employee who's been with the company eight to ten years, and the manager feels this employee is becoming less motivated or burned out. They're not sure how to help him, but they don't want to fire him as they've invested a lot of time and money in him. This person also has expertise that they need, but they're not getting the production they were used to seeing from him.

I can come in and do some counseling with the employee, do some work with his fellow workers and try to get this employee re-motivated, re-integrated.

Or maybe there's a squabble going on in the organization. Two factions or two sub-work groups don't work together well, and the manager has done all he can do and is unable to bring them together. I can come in and do some things to get them to work together.

I enjoy the balance that the diversity of my work brings.

GETTING THE CLIENT RESULTS

There are many consultants out there who will go in and do surveys, come back, write up a report and present it to the client. Ninety percent of those get shelved.

I don't do that.

I make the client do the work.

I have a philosophy—that they will get more out of it if they do most of the work. Now, just saying that, immediately someone is going to say they're going to resent paying me. But the fact is that they want the results and if I can help them get the results they want, they're going to be happy to pay me. They do the work, I guide them through it and they get the results they want.

My approach to management consulting is from the team's side. I'm part of the team. I go in and I'm with you. We have a working relationship; we collaborate on the problem together and we collaborate on the solutions

"He just persevered, and didn't let failure get in his way of being successful."

"We collaborate on

the problem together,

and we collaborate on

the solutions to-

gether."

together. Sometimes this is more painful for people because I raise questions that may be uncomfortable for them to confront. It's the same thing as the Toastmaster experience. You don't overcome your problem until you confront it.

A MATTER OF TRUST

I think I've probably modeled myself after my father. He's very easy going, very gentle and very supportive. He has a million friends in the furniture industry (his profession), and he's been a president of his professional group in Southern California for a number of years. He is widely respected in his field.

I think I learned a great secret from my father: "You may not personally obtain everything you would like, but if you're easy going, gentle and supportive, people will always trust you, rely on you and want to associate with you because they don't feel threatened; they feel comfortable."

STRONG AND GENTLE WINS

I think if people are doing what they want to be doing, having fun at it, and are accomplishing the things they want to accomplish, they are being successful. As long as people understand that there are going to be failures along the road, and they are patient but at the same time persistent with themselves, they will be successful. I feel I am.

When I was in therapy a number of years ago, the therapist said to me, "Only the strong can be gentle." That is a phrase that has stayed with me in everything I do in business. I understand that if I want to be strong and portray a strong image to people, I don't have to shove it down their throats. I don't have to beat the competitor to death; in fact, I can be gentle and encourage the competitor to be successful. He will return the favor. That's been a strong current in my life.

Steven D. Pomerantz
Professional Counseling Group of Sacramento
3336 Bradshaw Road, Suite 320
Sacramento, CA 95827
916-366-9483

Julie Pulos is president of Pacific Access Computers Inc., one of the nation's largest value-added resellers of AT&T computer systems. Ms. Pulos has a bachelor's degree in economics from the University of San Francisco and formerly was a licensed stockbroker with Dean Witter.

Pacific Access Computers is a thriving Rancho Cordova-based firm started just four years ago by Julie and Dennis Pulos. Selling AT&T, Unysis, Stratus and Sun Products as a value-added reseller is the primary function of this market-driven corporation, but it is now focusing on the engineering of systems integration solutions as a fast-growth area for the firm.

Although its services are not limited to the expanding telecommunications industry, the company has garnered its fair share of the Bell companies' business, with Pacific Bell as one of its major customers. Other members of PAC's client base include Fortune 100 companies, as well as all levels of state, federal and local government.

The business was started as a result of a known, yet unfulfilled, need within the newly deregulated telecommunications industry to make a product that fit the customers' needs rather than forcing customers to restrict their objectives to an existing product.

That was the initial concept and it remains true today, as the Puloses watch revenues soar from $700,000 in their first year to $16 million in 1989.

The underlying reasons for the early success of the company are the combined and complementary talents of Dennis and Julie. Dennis had the sales experience and futuristic vision to get the business rolling, while Julie had the financial and operational abilities to establish the organization and keep it running at an efficient and profitable level.

"What I brought to the business were strong operations and financial skills."

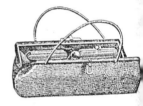

Author's Note: *If any two people set the standard for the "ma and pa" business of the 1990s, they are Julie and Dennis Pulos. They have been married for twelve years*

"Dennis brings strong sales capabilities to the business."

and are the proud parents of two young children. Juggling the demands of family with an emerging business may seem like an impossible task, but after spending a couple of hours with Julie and her limitless energy, it's easy to see she is a woman in command of her business and her life in general.

D ennis and I developed the basic concept for our business from a firm for which Dennis used to work, where he was hired to establish an advanced systems sales group.

He introduced a marketing approach and did an analysis of what markets the firm should be pursuing. Through that research, we saw a great need in the telecommunications industry. We said, "We can make these boxes bigger, better, stronger and mold the products around the customer needs instead of just throwing the products at the customer and telling him, 'Do whatever you can with it.'"

That was a phenomenal concept, and it worked. The people for whom Dennis worked had a personal computer mentality and didn't apply the concept to what we saw as its fullest potential. With that philosophy in mind, we left to start our own company.

We started the business in 1985. What I brought to the business were strong operations and financial skills. Since I was a stockbroker for several years and Director of Operations in a financial planning firm, these were not minor attributes. My degree in economics brought that expertise to the business as well.

Dennis brings strong sales capabilities to the business. He's been in sales for probably ten years now, the majority of it in the office equipment environment—especially computers.

THE HOT MARKETS

Most of the big computer systems you've seen are shrinking to small workstations. Networking is very big, and that has become our forte, as we're networking and communications specialists. We will go out, perform a user-needs analysis for customers to pinpoint their problems, and if we see a need, we will fill it by designing and developing a solution customized for them. We also sell hardware and provide whatever else the customer needs in that line.

I am in the process of setting up a leasing company that will be attractive, because now we can offer an alternative to the customer. We have training programs and seminars we're establishing and newsletters which are going out. We have a lot of new and exciting things going on!

THE TELECOM TRIO

We have three vertical markets: the telephone companies—both regulated and unregulated, the Fortune 100 firms and the government—state, local and federal. Within those markets our primary niche is telecommunications.

We provide hardware and software. We provide canned packages if they are needed, or we'll put together a whole networking package for our customers.

We have about $1 million invested in our development lab right now, and that's where we do demos, developments, and porting capabilities for customer problem solving. We have a full line of products from our suppliers—Sun, AT&T, Stratus and Unysis.

FIRST YEAR SETBACKS

The hardest part of getting our business off the ground was getting people to believe in us. I had to do a lot of selling to financial institutions, and if you don't have three years of financial history—a track record—they don't want to talk to you. Of course, now they're all coming to us, wanting our business.

We couldn't even get the major suppliers to take us seriously at first. They said, "Hey, go somewhere else. You're too small." No one would listen to us. Finally we found a large distributor and we told them, "We want to buy products from you." Fortunately, they were happy to sell them to us because they realized we knew more about the product line than they did. They had the money and the warehouses, and we had the knowledge.

Once we obtained the product, things started going a little bit better. In our first year we should have been doing $20 million, but we ran into complications with securing delivery of the products.

"We are in the process of setting up a leasing company that will be attractive, because now we can offer an alternative to the customer."

"We have about $1

million invested in our

development lab right

now..."

A PRIVATE AFFAIR

To accomplish what we wanted to accomplish that first year, we would have needed $4 to $5 million to start.

We decided to remain a private company and grow more slowly instead of going public to raise the capital. In one way it is good, because we own the company, but looking at it another way, we could have owned the market. Now we have a few competitors out there.

Since we have established ourselves, though, and drawing upon my past experiences in the brokerage industry, I don't see a public offering in our future. We may be bought someday or acquired by a large firm, but we're not corporate-structured people. We feel that to account to stockholders is just too much.

PERSPECTIVES ON SUCCESS FROM JULIE PULOS
- $1 million in R&D
- Employee importance
- Closely held stock
- Talk in plain English
- Minority/Woman-Owned Business

STRATEGIES FOR GROWTH

Our growth has been tremendous since our inception, going from sales of $700,000 our first year to $16 million in four years. There are several factors that have contributed to this growth.

First, we strategize. I make sure that we have managers' meetings as well as office meetings monthly. Our employees are very dedicated to us, and we structure a team effort, using that approach throughout our entire operation.

We have set up compensation packages so that everybody is involved, and management as well as support staff are integral parts of the company. I like to use the management philosophy that each employee is just as important to us as the next one.

FINDING THE EXPERTISE

The biggest challenge I see right now is finding the right people. We need key people who have enough training to take responsibility in their area almost immediately. I'm not saying we don't train, but our employees have to bring certain expertise to the team. We need to continue to focus on providing the best service to our customers.

TRAITS OF THE TEAM

Dennis handles the management of our sales force with salespeople we hire all coming from engineering backgrounds. Dennis looks for people who are courteous. He also looks at their background, how they were raised as children and how they live now. He does his job differently from most people. He knows how he was raised, and he knows what he's gone through to get where he is now. He knows why people deal with him, also he knows why they don't. He hires people in his own image. He looks for people who have had similar experiences to his, and who have the same types of beliefs that he has. That way he feels confident they will go out and do the same type of job.

We will never let the salespeople dedicate one hundred percent of their time to one customer because then they're forgetting about the rest of the world. If you put all of your eggs in one basket, sooner or later that basket is going to break.

All of our salespeople are required to make twenty new phone contacts per day. It's mandatory. There's always someone out there whom you've never met, and there is the distinct possibility of selling him something that will help him.

We look for engineers who can speak plain English, as there are a lot of them who will completely lose you after thirty seconds. They'll talk way over your head, and we have to have people that can translate technical jargon into understandable language. Good communications skills and drive are the prerequisites for our sales force. They have to have these basics in order to mold them into what we need and want.

NEVER SAY NO

I think success comes from having goals, number one, and from having the ambition to attain them—no matter what it takes. I operate in a role of "get in and get it done," and I'm sure if you talk to my employees, they will tell you that they understand how I operate. If I delegate something, it should be done right and according to my expectations. I've always been accountable for my actions as I believe everyone should be.

My first sense of being driven came to me when I was hired by a stock brokerage firm as a secretary. I told the manager at the time that I wanted to get my license.

"The hardest part of getting our business off the ground was getting people to believe in us."

"We couldn't even get the major suppliers to take us seriously at first. They said 'Hey, go somewhere else. You're too small.'"

He kind of shrugged it off and said, "You'll never do it. Every secretary wants to go for her license. You're just like all of the rest of them. You'll never make it."

I said, "Okay, fine." Then I took the books home and I studied every night after work because there were about thirty books. Two or three months later I went in and I said, "Okay, I'm ready to take the test." He just about fell off his chair!

When people tell me I can't do something, they inadvertently give me even more incentive. I view it as a challenge.

FRIENDS AND CUSTOMERS

This company is very customer oriented. We make sure that our employees understand that the customer comes first. When we do our organizational chart it's always funny because at the top of our chart is our customer. That way everyone knows that it's not Dennis and me or anyone else within the company up there—it's "our customer."

Dennis has a favorite motto—"You don't treat a customer like a customer, you treat a customer as a friend." You research their needs and where they want to be in the future. A lot of inner workings are revealed, and this brings you closer. Sometimes your customers don't even realize what they want until you pinpoint their problems and give them your solutions.

A PRODIGIOUS PAIR

Dennis is the dreamer who has the overall vision of what he wants. He receives a lot of feedback from his customers, and that's great. Then we sit down and I'm the one who actually implements our programs from an operations standpoint. This plan works out well because our paths don't cross very often. He doesn't want to have anything to do with operations—I can't even get him to sign an expense report!

That's what works out great. I'm the realist, he's the dreamer, and that's why we've been successful—both in business and in our twelve-year marriage. Sometimes it's hard with two small children, but fortunately, we have a great family, with both sets of our grandparents here. Our parents also live here and have been more than a help in caring for the kids.

MINORITY BENEFITS

Pacific Access is a minority/woman-owned business enterprise because I own sixty percent of it, with Dennis owning forty percent. We derive some benefits from structuring the business this way.

Certain agencies—such as the Public Utilities Commission and federal government agencies—have tried to give minorities equal opportunity in business. They give incentives and certain benefits to companies that do business with minority or woman-owned firms.

There have been advantages for us as we receive incremental business because we are a minority/woman-owned company. It is an "oh by-the-way" factor, because we don't use it to close a sale. It's just another bonus we provide for the customer.

MOVING TO THE NEXT PLATEAU

When you first start out in business you have to do a lot of hard selling while bending over backward to please people. Now we have established a track record, reached the first plateau, so to speak. We've made it past the statistics and now we have the capital as well as the financial structure to take it to the next plateau. However, it has to be done effectively.

Dennis is great because he has all the creative ideas. On my side of the coin, I've given up marketing and sales, but I support the whole infrastructure of the company, doing all of the forecasting. I know exactly how best to move money if we need to concentrate on research and development, if we want to put together a compensation package for the employees or if we need to create a new department. That's my stronghold, and I think that's why we work so well together, because he foresees the major goals and objectives while I put it together.

Julie Pulos
Pacific Access Computers Inc.
2945 Kilgore Road
Rancho Cordova, CA 95670
916-635-9300

"To accomplish what we wanted to accomplish that first year, we would have needed $4 to $5 million to start."

Bobby D Rinkle

Bobby Rinkle *is owner of Creative Impressions, a firm that specializes in custom artwork and limited editions for corporate offices. He is an accomplished artist, specializing in pastels, and formerly was an interior plant tech designer with The Tropical Glass House.*

F rom the etchings of early cave dwellers to today's
creative artists, mankind has always benefited
from chronicling important issues depicting
both cultural growth and change on canvas, cloth, wood
or stone.

Art captures one's attention like no newscast can,
communicating, not with voice or words, but through
symbols that reach into the crevices of our souls. It
evokes feelings about such subjects as nuclear fear, the
endangered environment, media pervasiveness and the
search for human values in this age of information.

Art has a natural place in our business lives as well,
as more and more business executives are replacing
twenty-dollar prints with serious art collections. Not only
is collecting art a good investment, it also provides an
attractive, stimulating environment for employees and
communicates a company's commitment to supporting
the arts within the community.

Bobby Rinkle is an avid promoter of interior plant
design and contemporary art in the Sacramento area. He
provides his clients with visual displays with such a flair
that they can tastefully spice up the most stuffy, overly
serious corporate setting.

An artist in his own right, Rinkle is satisfied with
representing regional artists and hanging their "pieces," as
he likes to call them, in strategic spots in many of
Sacramento's elite corporate offices.

"Executives are

learning that plants

accomplish much more

than just pleasing the

eye with their aesthetic

appeal."

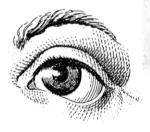

Author's Note: *Bobby is fortunate in that
he operates his business from his home,
where, as you would expect, I discovered
living room walls adorned with paintings,*

metal sculpture and paper art from his artists. Bobby is a delight. He has a "go for it" attitude—no stops, full steam ahead—and he is not shy about promoting himself and his artists. His love for art and plants and how the combination can enhance the image of a business is second only to his enthusiasm for people.

I view Sacramento right now as a super boom town. New offices are popping up overnight. Every one of these offices needs some kind of interior design, and most firms demand that plants be included in that design. The reason? Executives are learning that plants accomplish much more than just pleasing the eye with their aesthetic appeal. They enhance health in the office environment by consuming carbon dioxide and releasing oxygen. Even small plants can make the air cleaner in those little cubicles where many people work these days.

Plants also act as subliminal morale boosters because people love fresh plants, especially tropical plants. The combination of beautiful plants and tasteful artwork can really enhance the atmosphere and make people feel good, even though they may not consciously be aware of the effect.

In that sense, Creative Impressions is really designed to make people happy. Our methods center on art and plants, but our real job is to spread happiness throughout the office!

THE SEEDS OF CHANGE

All of this interest in enhancing the beauty of an office may sound strange coming from a former diesel mechanic. I guess it took the dingy atmosphere of the garage to make me realize that I wanted something more out of life.

The design business evolved from my interest in landscaping as I had been doing outdoor landscaping for quite a long time. I'm not really sure what the roots of that desire were (no pun intended), I have just always liked plants and the outdoors.

After leaving the diesel shop, I took some horticulture classes, studying outdoor landscaping and irrigation. I wanted to get into the design end of the business, but you have to start out at the bottom and work your way up.

In the summer, I started laying sod in one hundred degree temperatures, which is very hard and sweaty work. It didn't take me too long to realize that I didn't want to be outdoors all the time! Finally, I went to work for The Tropical Glass House, an interior design plant company, and there I found my niche.

"I started in the summer, laying sod in one hundred degree temperatures."

STONE-THROWING IN THE GLASS HOUSE

My career began on a part-time basis, prepping plants for the Glass House's office accounts. I would then take the new plants to offices around town and exchange them for the older ones. Soon I realized that even with very little experience, I seemed to have the ability to make plants grow—it just came naturally.

Eventually, the owners realized I was good at caring for the plants and promoted me to on-site plant maintenance for a few accounts. Almost overnight, my commitment ballooned from four hours a week to ten or twelve hours because we were pulling in so many new accounts.

After two years of learning, I was ready to begin designing—determining the types of plants and placements for new office accounts. The shop had a full-time designer and, although I thought there was plenty of work to go around, the owner of the company didn't see it the same way.

Thus the idea of starting my own business began to germinate. At first, I was reluctant to take all the risks associated with going it alone, as I had a wife and a child to support.

CONFIDENCE IN THE FORM OF A CASSETTE

Then, something unique happened, something that changed my life. I was watching TV late one night, specifically a show which featured several people discussing the wonderful change they had made in their lives. They had all purchased a series of tapes called *How To Build A Winning Self-Image* by Jonathan Parker.

At that time in my life, I was almost completely broke and feeling quite depressed about my career, but I ordered the tapes anyway. I thought I would check them

"These (cassette)

tapes helped me feel

good about myself and

taught me to give

others the benefit of

the doubt, both

personally and in

business."

out and probably return them in thirty days for my money back.

I kept the tapes. They were phenomenal. Right away they had an amazing impact on me. They taught me that I was just as good as anyone else, that I didn't have any reason to be intimidated by the professional types I'd been working with, even though I might be less educated than they. The cassettes taught me that I can pursue anything, and that I can accomplish anything I put my mind to. It sounds like a cliché, of course, but it took someone telling me this to really pound the truth of it into my head.

The tapes also showed me how my own negative thinking was rubbing off on other people. Mainly, I was depressed a lot of the time by my financial situation, and that was affecting the people around me. My mistrust of others was showing, too. These tapes helped me feel good about myself and taught me to give others the benefit of the doubt, both personally and in business. That ended my negative thinking!

PERSPECTIVES ON SUCCESS FROM BOBBY RINKLE
- Everything blooms in a boom
- Subliminal morale boosters
- Roots of desire
- A winning self image
- Art as investment
- Happy people are good referrals

BALANCING NAGLE WITH THE NARCISSUS
Right after receiving the tapes, I started thinking about marketing strategies for a new business. I knew that ideas for new businesses and new niches in the marketplace usually come from considering your own areas of expertise. I ended up realizing that, my gosh, I know several artists, as well as photographers and people who work in art galleries. Why not put those connections to work?

During my plant maintenance years, I was very aware of paintings and photographs set next to the plants, and I always judged their effects. Did the painting highlight the strong characteristics of the plant? Did the photograph and the plant harmonize, add something unique to the space?

I had been unconsciously training to design the perfect office, and when I opened my own business I did just that. That's how, in 1988, Creative Impressions was born.

A CREATIVE CONTRACT

One of the things I continually have to explain to new clients is that artwork, like plants, has a value beyond aesthetics. It is really an excellent investment, especially the way we do things.

We sign a contract with every new client, stating that we will come back within a ten-year period to make lithographs from any original painting we sell. By selling a limited number of the lithographs—or prints, as most people call them—we can increase the value of the original painting by as much as five hundred percent. The client will still own the painting and retain the rights to it, of course, but if he ever wants to sell it, he's required to give Creative Impressions the first option to buy.

Since we make an effort to buy only first quality artwork, having a building interior designed by us can be a real investment in the future. It's not uncommon for our paintings to triple in value within two or three years.

THE VALUE OF HAPPINESS

When I'm able to make the client happy and make the client's employees happy, I feel I've been successful. Of course I want to make money, but that is not my main concern.

My objective is to do a quality job, and in the end, pleasing my customers will translate into financial success, because I will keep their business. If they are happy, as well as satisfied with our efforts, they will come back to me—and they do!

GETTING PERSONAL

Personal contact is important to keeping my business alive. Many people mistakenly underrate it. In this type of endeavor, personal contact is a matter of being diplomatic. For instance, if I go out to an office and there's a conference going on, I know how to be discreet. I take care of my plants, get in and get out. More often than not, people want you to come in and they will say, "Hi, how is your day going?" They're looking for a little relief from the daily chores.

This is a service business, after all, with a big part of it providing the personal contact that I think more should provide. Any situation becomes boring if there is just a strict business relationship, with no room for rapport among people.

"I was very aware of paintings and photographs set next to the plants, and I always judged their effects."

"I had been unconsciously training to design the perfect office."

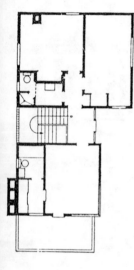

I handle many large facilities, such as the National Call Center for Federal Express and the Capitol Bank of Commerce. There are anywhere from two hundred to fourteen hundred plants in each of these facilities. That's a lot of plants, and it takes a lot of time to maintain them, but I never let myself feel so busy that I can't take the time to chat with people.

I think one key to success is allowing people to like you. Not making them like you, but just giving them the chance. My advice is to always take the time to say, "Hello," no matter how busy you are. It'll come back to you in the end.

PASSING ALONG THE CREATIVE WORD

One of my strengths as a businessman is networking. Of course, I'm not going to do something that will not be financially rewarding, but I don't think about money when I first meet a potential client. Instead, I think about how I'm going to make them happy—how I'm going to meet their needs.

That approach generally results in positive responses from the people I meet. They get to know me—I get to know them. That can be very beneficial, because word of mouth is the best advertising in the world. Even if they don't use my services, I ask them to mention my name to others. I've had a lot of business from referrals that way.

KEEPING THE RIGHT PERSPECTIVE

I often find myself thinking, "Gosh, I wish I had a thousand clients" or "I wish I had my own gallery right now." Then I realize how far I've come in two years and I feel I've accomplished a lot.

Two-and-a-half years ago I was working for someone else. Since then, I've built my own business by my own sweat and energy, and it's successful. You know, hey, I've made it a long way!

The important thing is to believe in yourself. With self-belief and a lot of persistence, success will happen quite naturally.

Bobby Rinkle
Creative Impressions
6220 Longdale Drive
North Highlands, CA 95660
916-334-3206

Tom Sartoris
is founder and president of Career Associates Inc. He has a bachelor's degree in science and education from Purdue University and a master's degree in counseling psychology from Arizona State University. He is also a certified rehabilitation counselor and a registered vocational expert. Sartoris is a member of the National Rehabilitation Counseling Association and the California Association of Rehabilitation Professionals. In addition, he is a California NARPPS board member.

T oday, many managers and business owners are faced with increasing numbers of profit-sapping human resource issues. Perhaps there is a high turnover rate within the sales staff or a company hires experienced secretaries only to find that their skills are not up to par.

"I firmly believe ethics contain the key to establishing and building a business."

Fortunately, professional help is available. Under the experienced guidance of founder Tom Sartoris, Career Associates Inc. provides vocational evaluations, job analyses and job placements which enable employers to solve these productivity issues.

Career Associates has been labeled "the total employment solution" by some clients and "the human resource guidance counselor" by others. With offices in Sacramento, Modesto, Stockton and Placerville, the company has the staff and the expertise to handle—and avert—many of the problems facing employers today.

The company was built on the foundation of workers' compensation rehabilitation services. Perhaps the most fascinating part of the business is the demand for Sartoris as an expert vocational witness. In this capacity he is called to testify in a variety of legal situations. For example, his expert opinion may be called upon to determine an employee's limitations in the labor force after an accident or to testify regarding a spouse's employability during divorce proceedings.

In addition the firm handles pre-employment screening for employers, as well as offering testing and guidance for career development to individuals.

In the ten years since its inception, the company has been kept on a path of steady, well planned growth and expanding areas of expertise.

What are the requirements to be a member of Sartoris' team? To share his vision, his philosophy and his goal to continually excel in the profession.

"I wouldn't recom-

mend that anyone

launch a business the

way I did."

Author's Note: Tom Sartoris and I met for lunch at The Ram to get acquainted. Good food and excellent conversation about business in general, and Career Associates, in particular, led to this chapter being written.

I firmly believe ethics contain the key to establishing and building a business. I learned my own strict code of ethics from my parents. My father is one of the most honest human beings I know, having climbed the career ladder from fire fighter to assistant chief without compromising his values. He was faced with attempted bribes from people who wanted to manipulate the system, but he refused the tainted fast buck. He is the role model I used to build my business and define excellence within my organization.

A SLIM START

I wouldn't recommend that anyone launch a business the way I did. I lost my job with only five hundred dollars in my savings account, a desk, a phone and a typewriter that I rented for twenty-five dollars per month. I worked all the hours I could, doing anything and everything. Every check that came in went to my house payment, and my only transportation was a beat-up car that I bought for four hundred dollars.

I didn't leap blindly into the rehabilitation services business, however. Before starting my own operation, I was a director for both the Sacramento and Redding offices of a nationwide rehabilitation services firm, supervising a staff of nine, and directing administration, marketing and training. I also did consulting, counseling, testing, placement, research and testimony. I did my homework before I decided to go it alone.

AN EXPLOSIVE EDUCATION

I have the kind of diverse background that has helped me prosper on my own. I received my bachelor's degree from Purdue University with a double major in general science and elementary education. I started out in pre-med until I realized that I didn't enjoy being diagnostic and science oriented. I'm much more interested in helping people. Once I accidentally created a chemical explosion in class.

This helped me decide to put my education degree to work and leave the science back at the lab!

After a year in the educational system, teaching sixth grade, I decided I didn't like the politics required in order to teach in the public schools. I went back to college and earned a master's degree in psychological counseling from Arizona State University in Tempe.

MIXED SIGNALS

By the time I started my first job in rehabilitation counseling in 1975, I had racked up a lot of related experience in youth and family counseling at Maricopa County Youth Service Bureau in Arizona, as well as psychological counseling at Arizona State Hospital.

The following year at age twenty-six, the company I was working for promoted me to director of rehabilitation services for Sacramento and Redding. I remained there for five years, but I grew tired of the capricious demands. One day they wanted someone who was independent and a self-starter, the next they wanted a company person.

I realized that I couldn't do my best work there, nor could I meet my major career objective—to serve people seeking help. I wanted to believe things would change, but when they didn't, I learned an important lesson— sometimes you have to let go. In business and personal relations you can't move on without letting go of the past. I wanted to start my own business so I could better serve clients, and I wanted to do this without a chain of command. It wasn't possible to enact the changes I felt were needed for my clients in my former job; there were too many roadblocks and empty promises.

In March 1980, the company shut down its Redding office, and cut the Sacramento staff down to two. Although I wasn't one of the remaining people, I do believe that if you haven't been fired at least once in your life, you haven't attempted to initiate enough change. Employers can't expect to hire self-starters who are independent thinkers and doers, then turn around and expect them to become yes men. You can't change a leopard's spots.

FROM TESTIMONY TO TRAINING

In the ten years since I started Career Associates, Inc., it has grown from a single purpose company that counseled a client base of three companies on workers' compensa-

"Once, I accidentally created an explosion in class. This helped me decide to put my education degree to work and leave the science back at the lab!"

"One day they wanted someone who was independent and a self-starter, the next they wanted a company person."

tion claims, to a multifaceted organization that has expanded into new and related areas.

I have become an expert witness on vocational issues involving personal injury cases. I offer testimony on what the plaintiff can't do and in other cases what the defendant can do. Through research and interviews, I learned the limitations and strengths of clients, and then showed them how they could be productive and self-reliant in spite of their injuries.

I also act as a vocational expert witness in divorce cases involving spousal support, evaluating a spouse to determine career options and make recommendations.

In another branch of my work, I perform skills assessments for employers. For example, I will prescreen a group of people an employer is considering hiring. I also teach employers how to select the best employees and how to devise job descriptions.

Career guidance and vocational testing for the general public is a new area into which I am just beginning to venture. While I am still undergoing feasibility testing, I think career guidance in a seminar format has dynamic possibilities. I'm looking at the type of large scale counseling that would reach many people and make my fees affordable. I realize, however, that ethically, I could be treading on sensitive ground if I don't handle it properly. I don't want it to be viewed as a get-rich-quick scheme, because it's not.

PERSPECTIVES ON SUCCESS FROM TOM SARTORIS
- Fighting fires with integrity
- Expert testimony
- Quality-first traits
- Taking risks
- Low key marketing
- Keeping the vision

LENDING AN EAR TO THE COMMUNITY
In addition to running my business, I do a lot of community work. I have a track record of helping the low-income people and the needy. I donate office services to churches and nonprofit groups. For people who can't afford my career guidance services, I charge less than half of my regular fee to help get them off the ground. It's a way to give something back to the community.

A WINNING PHILOSOPHY, A WINNING TEAM

In nine years my business has grown to the point that I now require four counselors, two job developers and counseling assistants, and four people to perform administrative and clerical work. I think of my business in terms of a "team concept." A "family" is too personal and corny. My objective is to ensure that Career Associates is a safe place to work and a safe place for clients to come. It is necessary that we get along with each other and work as a cohesive team. Our offices have to be safe for our clients who are already having problems in their lives.

As a team, we must share the same vision and the same dream, head toward the same goals. Our philosophy and ethics must be in alignment. We must have all of this in order to provide a service to help people.

This office is unique because of the talents of the people, who all have integrity and strong ethics. We try not to overburden ourselves with a large number of cases, or to just work toward achieving a money goal.

I look for employees who possess the "quality-first" trait. If they have quality, then I can help them become more productive. If an employee isn't motivated by quality, the success of the business is short term, and I want long term.

RISKY BUSINESS

The biggest obstacle I had to overcome in building my business was to force myself to take risks. Letting go of safe feelings and spending the money to move on was difficult. Looking back, I think I should have done it years ago—quit my job and started my own firm. On the other hand, I learned a lot from my past employers about how to run a business like this and how not to do it.

REWARDING HIGHLIGHTS

The reward of building Career Associates has been the great sense of accomplishment. Seeing positive results, having a philosophy and improving it to see that it does work is great. Your own business also allows flexibility, especially in structuring your time. If a personal matter or business choice takes me away during regular business hours, I can opt to make it up by working evenings or weekends. I am making more money now than I've ever made before, but that's the secondary reward. The freedom to make changes and to organize my own time is

"In business and personal relations you can't move on without letting go of the past."

"Employers can't expect to hire self-starters who are independent thinkers and doers, then turn around and expect them to become yes-men."

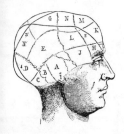

at the top of the reward scale. There's no flexibility in working nine-to-five as a corporation puppet.

CONFIDANTS AND COMPANIONS

There are two people in my life who are a great help to me. Gary Sacco—one of them—is a man I hired in 1978, who eventually went on to start his own business. He has impacted my life in a very positive way. Then there is my wife, Janie, who is a special education teacher. She is very supportive, and my first priority in life as we begin to anticipate children in our future. Our marriage three years ago was the first for both of us. My most constant companion over the years has been Kaibab, my eleven-year-old, hundred-pound Great Pyrenees.

AN EDUCATION IN REALITY

I think education is vital to an entrepreneur. Whether it is from a college or the school of hard knocks is not important. My advice to anyone just graduating from business school is first to learn to work and live in the real world. There is no way that you can directly apply what you have learned in school to real life situations. You should also be willing to start at the bottom, working for someone else while you are in school or as soon as you graduate so reality isn't a shock.

A GENTLE MARKETING APPROACH

As with most businesses, marketing has been its lifeblood. Without new business and new clientele, the company would die. I think the best marketing tactic in the world is to do a good job. That way I don't have to do a lot of hardcore marketing. I don't believe in trying to be someone I'm not. You have to be yourself and not promise more than you can deliver.

I advertise in the Yellow Pages and I am considering a few other areas. For businesses like mine, business cards and the telephone are the two most important marketing tools, yet I still tend to look at myself as a counselor instead of a businessman.

SUCCESSFUL GOALS

The success of my business is directly related to the success of my personal relationships. Being humble as well as trying to make sure the customer is never wrong has helped me prosper. It's important to be tactful and diplomatic when providing a service.

Goals are an important factor to success. However, I think goals should be carefully thought out and flexible. I have personal goals—short, medium and long-term—but I adjust them to the changing times.

What's really important is to keep the vision always in mind. It's like a plane as it flies from San Francisco to New York. It must constantly readjust its course due to the wind, weather and other factors. The course isn't one straight line.

My personal goal, besides staying in business, is to expand my organization to its fullest extent. I think that by diversifying, Career Associates will have increased balance and security—two things we all need in our lives!

Tom Sartoris
Career Associates Inc.
3716 Marconi Avenue
Sacramento, CA 95821
916-486-9777

"I do believe that if you haven't been fired at least once in your life, you haven't attempted to initiate enough change."

Alice Thomas is the proprietor of *River Rose Country Inn, a bed and breakfast establishment located in the heart of Freeport. Ms. Thomas and her husband Albert operate the Inn with help from their friends and associates.*

In the past year, seventy-year-old Alice Thomas has embarked on the most challenging venture of her life—the River Rose Country Inn. It wasn't a matter of merely having the rooms of a home renovated or finding the financing to purchase a completed inn. Alice literally started her business from the ground up—choosing the site, the architect, the builder, the investors and the mortgage to put it all together. The result is a beautifully quaint ten room bed & breakfast inn, which opened on January 1, 1990 in the sleepy town of Freeport, California. A warm feeling surrounds anyone entering the cozy Thomas establishment, having much more than the comforts of home. The eclectic decor is enhanced by the relaxing double hot tubs in each room. Guests will find they can enjoy a romantic dinner at the inn, as well as the customary breakfast.

Situated in a rural setting lush with greenery, the River Rose has already attracted the attention of couples seeking a convivial setting for weddings, as well as ministers seeking comfortable lodging for religious retreats.

As quaint and sedate as the inn is, its proprietor is anything but. Alice Thomas is not a retired, wealthy matriarch looking for a project to keep her busy in her golden years. Instead, she is an energetic, no-nonsense type of busineswoman who took on the laborious task of erecting the first new building of the century in Freeport. The River Rose Country Inn is not a dalliance; it is Alice's way of ensuring the income she will need in her retirement.

True, she is already of the age which finds most people quietly sitting, looking back in reflection, but this lively woman has no intention of settling down. Along with her husband Albert, Alice has plans for many more

"Enough is enough.

You can't just keep digging a grave for yourself with problems."

"I have loved roses since I was in junior high school. I grew up in Santa Rosa where roses lined many of the parkways."

challenges and successful ventures in her lifetime. Perhaps she will consider retirement in another twenty years!

Author's Note: *I first met Alice at the construction site of the River Rose Inn in the fall of 1989. She proudly gave me a tour of her establishment, telling me of her decisions with regard to design and construction. With her opening less than a couple of months away, she was happy to see her dream coming alive. Later, as we sat and talked in the construction shed, which had been her home away from home for some time, I realized that the Inn was to be Alice's legacy. I'm pleased to add another chapter to that story.*

By the time I was sixty-two, I had been married, divorced, raised a family, and had several careers which involved a number of moves. Finally I landed in Sacramento where one day I found myself laid off from my job with a title company. Right then I said, "Enough is enough. You can't just keep digging a grave for yourself with problems."

I decided I'd take real estate courses and become a real estate salesperson. My dad—who was an optometrist—told me that when you have a state license, it proves that you've gone to school and learned the trade. It also means you're a qualified person, which gives you more self-esteem. He was right. I passed the exam and made nine sales in my first month!

That experience, combined with my knowledge of motel and construction company management, greatly helped to make the inn a reality.

WHAT'S INN A NAME

When we named our bed & breakfast River Rose Country Inn, all of our partners had input, but I must admit, it brought back happy memories for me.

I have loved roses since I was in junior high school. I

grew up in Santa Rosa where roses lined many of the
parkways. I remember a lady who would give me roses
to take to school with me every day.

Roses also remind me of my childhood summers. I
used to spend them on the Russian River where these
little flat, round, pink wild roses grew along the banks up
and down the river. I remember thinking they were so
pretty.

My husband Albert was the one who wanted "River"
in the name, and the name especially fits Freeport
because it is such a beautiful town. It's a sleeping future.
Al calls it the best antiquated village in California.

MEETING THE PERFECT MAN—FINDING THE PERFECT SPOT
I met my husband Albert on March 23, 1981 at the
Golden Tee Restaurant. Being married to him is one of
the crowning achievements in my life—the other being
my three children. He really stands behind me.

The idea for a bed & breakfast inn came to Al and
me after we were married and had the opportunity to
visit a few of them. We decided that it would be a neat
business for us because we could both take an active part
in it.

We first looked at sites in Yolo County and along the
Garden Highway and almost made the mistake of buying
a five-bedroom house by the airport. It was a good thing
we didn't because it was eventually flooded. We also
found out later that the residents living on the Garden
Highway are against commercialization.

In Yolo County, the officials know nothing about bed
& breakfast inns. We went to the county offices to find
out what their rules were, and they didn't have any.

Eventually, we decided to buy the old school in
Freeport for our inn, but because of septic system problems, the deal fell through.

Finally, in 1987—two years after we started talking
about it—we purchased a piece of property in Freeport
for $200,000. The inn was constructed for another
$700,000, and before it was even completed an MAI
appraisal valued the property at $1.4 million. I figure it
will be worth at least $2.5 million next time it's appraised.

A NON-VICTORIAN PARTNERSHIP
Once we found the property, we began searching for
partners by bringing the idea up at club meetings and

"The idea for a bed & breakfast inn came to Al and me after we were married and had the opportunity to visit a few of them."

"...we purchased a

piece of property in

Freeport for $200,000.

The inn was con-

structed for another

$700,000, and before

it was even completed

an MAI appraisal

valued the property at

$1.4 million."

business and professional women's meetings. We talked to as many people as we could. We talked to several contractors, attorneys and doctors, but none of these people bit. They just couldn't see it. They didn't understand what we were talking about it, and that we had the necessary experience.

We'd describe our bed & breakfast, but they thought it was just some old Victorian—not at all the inn we were about to build. Our inn would be a place where you could have a lovely garden wedding and comfortable lodging as well. I knew it would sell.

Finally, we met some people who caught our vision, and we ended up with five partners in a general partnership, with my vote being the final decision maker.

BIG BEAR ADVICE
Before we finalized our plans, I received some great advice from a fellow who owned a bed & breakfast inn in Big Bear, California. The best recommendation he gave was that "you need seven to ten rooms, but don't go over ten because then you can't control the operation." Controlling it means that you can visit with the people, and that's part of the PR work you do. The other important thing he said to do is to offer the guests dinner in their rooms and charge them. He even gave me his budget to follow.

My friends, Robin and Lyle, who ran the Ponderosa Hotel, also gave me good advice.

PERSPECTIVES ON SUCCESS BY ALICE THOMAS
- Stop and smell the roses
- Networking for partners
- Business advice
- Financing the project
- From dream to success
- Support from Albert

TOUGH FINANCING
We had everything we needed except the financing; the biggest hurdle we encountered was that of finding a lender who believed in us enough to loan us the money. We went to ten different lenders—including the Chamber of Commerce—and all turned us down. Female loan officers were much more open to the idea than men were. Men wouldn't go for the wedding chapel, for example,

because it's only used on the weekends.

Also bed & breakfast inns have been known to fold because they only have three or four rooms—a big problem, as my friend from Big Bear had said. The owners think they will make a little extra retirement money, and they go out and mortgage their place to redo an inn, then they end up not being able to make the payments because they don't have the clientele.

Finally, we met Jim Morgan through North Bay Mortgage, and he has been a tremendous help to us ever since.

He was the one who finally found somebody who would go with our idea. He's been a very high quality backup. If I have a question of should we do this, or should we do that, financially, I can call him. He doesn't tell me how to do it, he slides into it kind of back-doorish, but I know when I get through, there is the satisfaction of having the answer and knowing two or three ways to go. He's really outstanding as a lender.

"...the biggest hurdle we encountered was that of finding a lender who believed in us enough to loan us the money."

BUILDING QUALITY
The contractor we chose, Bob Fuhs, is also wonderful. Not only have I known his wife for twenty years, but I have seen the excellent quality of his workmanship. He's an outstanding builder who likes to take his time and do things right.

AN IRA FOR THOSE OVER 65
Retirement was the issue that motivated me to start this business. Al has a good pension because he worked for the state, but I don't have much money coming in. When I got my divorce years ago, women didn't receive any interest in their husband's retirement. All I had was the little bit from Social Security. When you're in sales you're self-employed, and the amount paid into Social Security determines the amount received at age sixty-two or sixty-five.

I really feel compelled to make this business work. I have never wanted to quit. At seventy, when I have a problem I say, "Hey, that's just another step forward, another day. We'll go on and do something different tomorrow. We'll figure another way to do it."

A ROSEY SUCCESS
It's beginning to dawn on me that the River Rose Country

"At seventy, when I

have a problem I say,

'Hey, that's just

another step forward,

another day. We'll go

on and do something

different tomorrow.'"

Inn is a success! It's just beginning to get there and it's nice to have that feeling of accomplishing something this big—to finish it without dropping the ball.

Believing has kept me going with this project, and that's what it takes in life.

THE FAST-TALKING CPA

We were considering hiring a CPA, so we had her come here to meet our partners. Not only did she overcharge, but she also talked way above our heads. We're not that kind of people. We're down to earth, in our funny groove, but we're all making it.

YOUTHFUL TIPS

For a young person who wants to own a business like this, my advice is to do your homework, some leg work and backup work—research it, and go to college. Study real estate and business law. Also, take a speed reading course so you can read more quickly to absorb things faster, and finally, learn something about computers because you need them in business today.

POLISH YOUR FAUCET

You have to cover all bases to spread the word about a business like this. We couldn't have done this project without all sides of the faucet being polished. They're being polished now. I booked one wedding as a result of the first mailer which will cover the entire cost of the mailer. We probably will hire a wedding consultant as a help for the brides in their wedding interviews. I will probably sit in on the first meeting to ensure the service we want to give is being provided. We even have the invitations printed at a discount. I love the weddings!

We are also hoping to book church retreats. It would be ideal for a small group because they could have the entire place for the weekend. We would pick people up at the airport and whatever else they might need.

We would still like to purchase the Freeport school too, since it's actually the only empty building in Freeport that could be used for a wedding chapel, and I think it would enhance Freeport's image.

CONSERVATIVE DREAMS

I think I'm more of a conservative than I am a perfectionist, because I think you have to be a conscientious,
conservative person to dream, to build and to become
something. I definitely know that, in order to build a
quality thing, you can't be a liberal. You can't go out
there and play and not consider all of the aspects of what
you're doing.

FROM ALBERT'S VIEWPOINT

ALBERT: My dad always said he liked a woman with
some "get up" to herself. He'd like Alice. She's always
doing something. She's not the type to lie back, sit there
and watch television. That's why I married her—she has
"get up and go!"

> **Alice Thomas**
> **River Rose Country Inn**
> **8201 Freeport Blvd.**
> **Sacramento, CA 95832**
> **916-443-4248**

Allen Wong, D.D.S., operates a family dental practice in Roseville. In addition to his professional endeavors, Dr. Wong is also active in community affairs and has established a distinguished record of service to the Optimist Clubs in the Sacramento area.

tion to me and they both wanted me to be a doctor. With that goal in mind, they worked hard and did everything in their power to see that I made it through college and into dental school.

    I like to feel good, and it's nice to be wanted as well as needed. I love the feeling I get from doing something for someone else. I can't ever get enough of that great feeling! I think it is because my parents were so generous. Not only with money, but with love. To me, it's a celebration that I can give back to others what has been given to me. Without the generous support provided by my parents, grandmother, aunt and uncle in Louisiana, and a special friend, Mr. Benjamin Hudgens, I never would have achieved my goal as a dentist. I have been blessed with very supportive family and friends.

"...cost is never a consideration when I plan treatments."

A QUALITY TEACHER

There has been one other person important in shaping my career, and that is Dr. Kerry Hanson, who was an administrator at the clinic where I did my residency. He also has a private practice in the Roseville area. Dr. Hanson was very instrumental in opening my eyes to what quality dentistry is in the real world. Most of what he taught me was by example.

    His patients are enamored of him, and I assisted him in providing dental care to them. He's a man who cares intensely about his patients and people in general. He's happy with what he does, and that is precisely what I want to be.

STACKING THE DECK

I chose the University of the Pacific dental school for the same reason I chose its undergraduate program. The student-to-teacher ratio is great. The instructors were well-educated, very knowledgeable and willing to help.

    I felt I needed special attention because I didn't grow up with the same background or privileges as many of the other students. Since my parents didn't have a college education or a medical background to give me an anchor, I felt like I was going in without a full deck, so I needed the support from the instructors. They were superb people!

"It's not good enough to write a check and say, 'Here's so much for United Way.' You have to put not only your money where your mouth is—you have to put your hands there, too."

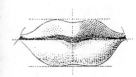

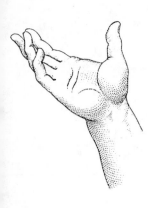

NO PEDALS ON THIS EQUIPMENT

There are always cheaper ways of doing things in dentistry. There are cheaper drills and cheaper anesthetics. A dentist who doesn't care about his patients can always make more money than one who cares, but cost is never a consideration when I plan treatments. I think that's one of the keys to business success—to be proud of what you do and be the best you can be.

Don't get me wrong, I'm not flawless. I realize that I'm not perfect, but as long as I keep trying to do the best I can and keep using the best quality tools and facilities available, I will continue to be proud of my work. Just having your patients know that you care is a lot of what Dr. Hanson imparted to me, and this is the way I run my business today.

STRANGERS IN THE NIGHT

In addition to my practice here, I work in Oakland at Highland General Hospital weekly. It's a hectic schedule and I hope to reduce my traveling considerably within one year, six months and two days. That's when my wife, Elizabeth, will complete her surgical residency at San Joaquin Hospital in Stockton. When she establishes her practice here, we will both be able to spend more time at our home in Roseville!

PERSPECTIVES ON SUCCESS BY ALLEN WONG

- The Optimist's Creed
- Lessons from Chinese immigrants
- Dental mentor
- Sacrifices of a professional couple
- Turning bad days into good
- Keeping kids off drugs

A LESSON FROM CHINA

I learned a long time ago that the more you get involved in the community, the more the community gets involved with you. It's not good enough to write a check and say, "Here's so much for United Way." You have to do something concrete to make this a better place to live. You have to put not only your money where your mouth is— you have to put your hands there, too.

I am part of a program sponsored by Roseville Community Hospital and the American Red Cross that teaches CPR to thousands of people in our community.

Participating in life-saving classes like these really makes our community so much tighter and stronger. I like to take part in local activities because I believe part of being a successful business person is being a generous contributor to the welfare of your community. That was ingrained in me by my parents. It's what made China a great country for thousands of years.

FRATERNIZING

When I was in college, the Alpha Phi Omega National Service Fraternity gave me a good forum to create service programs, develop membership programs, experiment with what I didn't know, run meetings, speak in front of groups and like doing it.

After I graduated and went to dental school, I enjoyed the fraternity so much that I remained involved on the sectional level. Two other chapters—one at San Francisco State and one at Hayward State—were rechartered due to my efforts. While everyone else was studying, I was working for a cause and studying at the same time.

It seemed that the more I did for the volunteer groups, the more energy I had to study. It really charged me up to provide volunteer service.

Obviously I didn't do it all alone, as some key people helped me out in the process. I strongly believe in leadership, friendship and service. I've grown tremendously and I've gained a lot of very good friends from it.

DON'T BE SHY

I love meeting people, which is a great boost to my business. It is my belief that in life you have to be able to communicate, to be able to find out what other people's needs are. I can't be an effective dentist by sitting back and acting shy. I have to be the kind of person who can go out and say, "Hi, how are you feeling?" and really care about the answer.

HOW TO BE AN OPTIMIST IN A WORLD OF (TOOTH) PAIN

The service I am most actively involved in right now is the Roseville Optimist Club. It's all about service to youth. It's an organization where we meet, raise money and support programs such as bicycle safety and "Just Say No." I think it's important because the youth of today are our future and we need to encourage them and to teach

"It seemed that the more I did for the volunteer groups, the more energy I had to study."

"...my patients love my

surprising promptness.

It doesn't happen often

in the medical or

dental world."

them that the good will prevail.

At the same time we are doing this, we're also trying to live up to a philosophy of optimism.

Basically, the philosophy says, "All right! Life is good!"

You promise yourself to be strong and to persevere through the hard times because things could be worse.

It's a good way to live. When I first came across the philosophy, I realized that living by this creed is something that I would love. Strength and perseverance are daily goals of mine.

Just seeing the words "Optimist's Creed" makes my day better. On days when I have problems, say a lot of patients don't show up for various reasons or my assistant is having a bad day, I can just go look at it and say, "Okay, let's start again." You have to count your blessings. There are many things that could have gone wrong today. You can either take it and cry about it, or you can accept it and try to build something positive from it.

BUILDING A PRACTICE WITH GOOD TIMING

My personal philosophy is that time is the most valuable thing we have in life. I think in this country we don't always respect each other as much as we should, and you have to respect each other's time. My expectations are that my patients will be here on time or early. As an incentive I tell them, "If you're here early and I'm finished with my previous patient, I will see you. I won't let you sit out there."

My goal for each patient, regardless of his monetary distinction, is to try to see him on time. I believe this is one definite practice-builder for me, and my patients love my surprising promptness. It doesn't happen often in the medical or dental world.

I have made it such a strong policy that I am willing to credit a patient's account for ten dollars if he waits more than twenty minutes. That doesn't happen very often, but I want to show them in good faith that I respect the fact that they are patiently waiting.

EXPERIENCING THE PAIN FIRST HAND

Nobody loves the dentist, or at least that's the myth. I've tried to get around that by learning to empathize with my patients. For instance, when you learn how to give shots in dental school, you do it on other dental students so you find out a great deal about empathy and pain.

There is a theory that dentists are not liked, and they sometimes internalize the stress that comes with the negative attention.

Fortunately, I'm able to channel my energies elsewhere. I accept the challenge when a patient sits in my chair and says, "Doctor, I hate coming to the dentist. I'm so afraid." I vow to turn that patient around so they walk away saying, "That wasn't so bad. I'll be back!" That is my goal for each patient.

"When you learn how to give shots in dental school, you do it on other dental students, so you find out a great deal about empathy and pain."

PR ASSISTANCE

If there's one key factor—other than the dentist himself—that makes a dental office thrive, it's the dental assistants. They're extremely important. The way they treat my patients determines whether they come back or not. My aides have to have faith in me. If your assistants don't think your work is good, that will brush off on the patients, but if they are proud of your work, it shows, too.

I think of all my employees as part of my team. I have to make sure they know what I'm doing, to make sure they're happy with what I do and proud of what I do because, darn it, we're going to do the best we can.

DENTISTRY IS NOT THE ROOT OF LIFE, MERELY THE FILLING

For me, being a successful dentist is not enough to make me feel personally fulfilled. I base my success on my role in the community. My participation in the Optimist Club is a good example of that. We're looking for people who are energetic and enthusiastic about helping the youth in our area. We want to make it better and keep our kids off drugs, maybe get them involved with the community if possible. We also want to raise money for the handicapped.

Bicycle safety is a big concern, too. We're getting more traffic in Roseville and we're going to have more car/bike accidents. Who's going to suffer from that? The children. Believe me, it's tough when you have to go a child's funeral—it's really tough. If we can be part of bicycle safety and prevent something like that, I think that's where we need to be.

We also try to develop civic mindedness, not only in the kids, but in each other. We talk about civic responsibility. We're trying to line up speakers that will enhance us in those areas—developing a good network of positive people, because we realize that if we, as a community, get together, we can accomplish a lot of good. We can make this place so much nicer and safer for everyone, kids and elderly alike. Dentistry is what allows me to be self-sufficient enough to participate in these activities—what I define as the most important aspect of life!

Allen Wong, D.D.S.
Family Dentistry
400 Sunrise Ave., Ste. C
Roseville, CA 95661
916-783-5144